Jessica Maloy

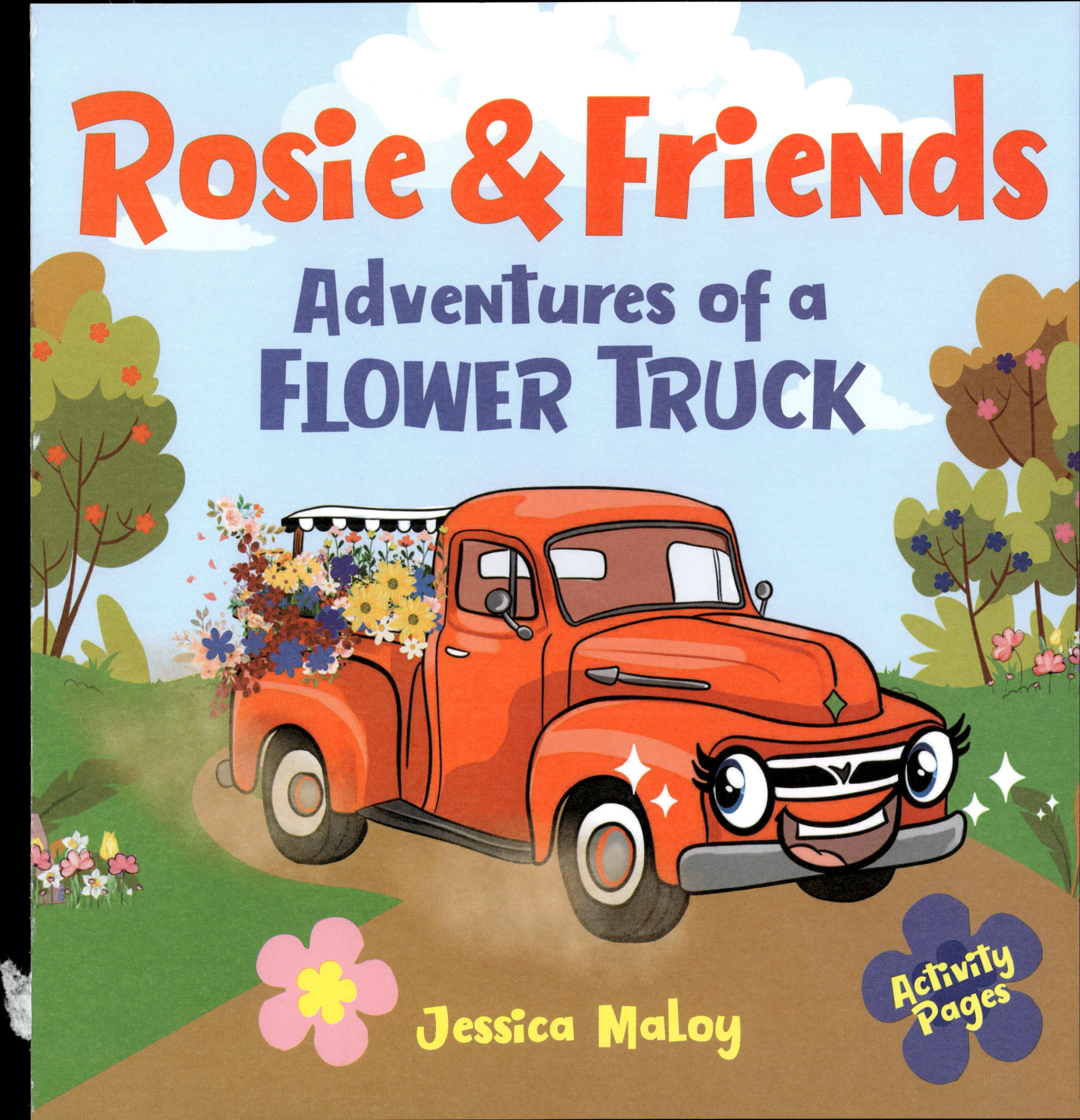

Rosie & Friends
Adventures of a FLOWER TRUCK

Jessica MaLoy

Activity Pages

Rosie & Friends, Adventures of a Flower Truck

ISBN 978-0-9994587-1-6
Printed in the United States of America

©2023 by Jessica Maloy
www.rosieandfriendsbook.com

Illustrations by Hancock Ghostwriters

CARACYN Publishing LLC
1205 Ridge Road
Grantville, PA 17028
717-469-7329
www.caracynpublishing.com

All rights are reserved. No part of this book may be reproduced or transmitted in any form or by any means, electronic or mechanical, including photocopying, recording, or by any information storage and retrieval system, without permission in writing from the publisher or author.

I dedicate this book to my family.

To my husband, Patrick.
You are always there to encourage me and my ideas.

To my son, Alex.
Thank you for being a light in my world.

To my mom, Corine.
You are there for me, always.

To my dad, Gary (Dibo) and father-in-law, Ed.
Thank you for the fun characters in my book.
I sure wish you were here to see it all.

To my mother-in-law, Rose.
Thank you for the use of your special name.
Not only does it fit our truck so well but it also
made Rosie and Eddie a good couple in the story.

To my extended family and friends.
Thank you all for the support and
for putting up with all
of my wild ideas.

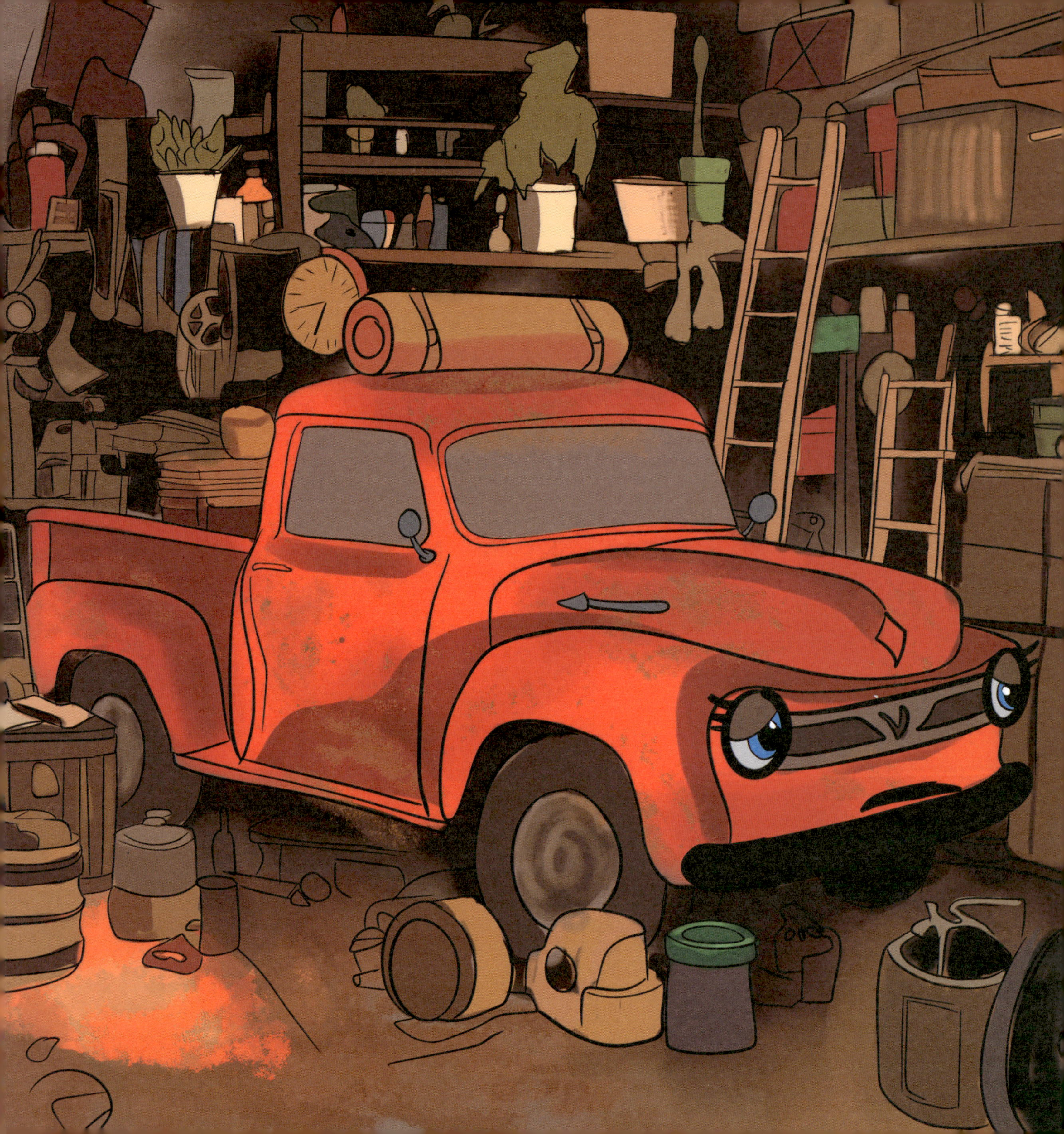

Rosie & Friends
Adventures of a FLOWER TRUCK

The old truck was very sad sitting in a cold, dark garage among cluttered papers, dirt, cobwebs, and old tires. She didn't drive anywhere, nobody talked to her, she just sat there quietly, all alone. Sunbeams shone on her smooth red paint through the small garage windows during the day and at night she was lucky if some moonbeams snuck in on her.

I'm a truck, she said to herself. *My wheels should be gliding down many kinds of roads, my horn should be honking 'hello' to people I pass by. What's out there beyond these garage doors? It's been so long since I've been outside in the fresh air and felt the hum of my engine. SIGH!*

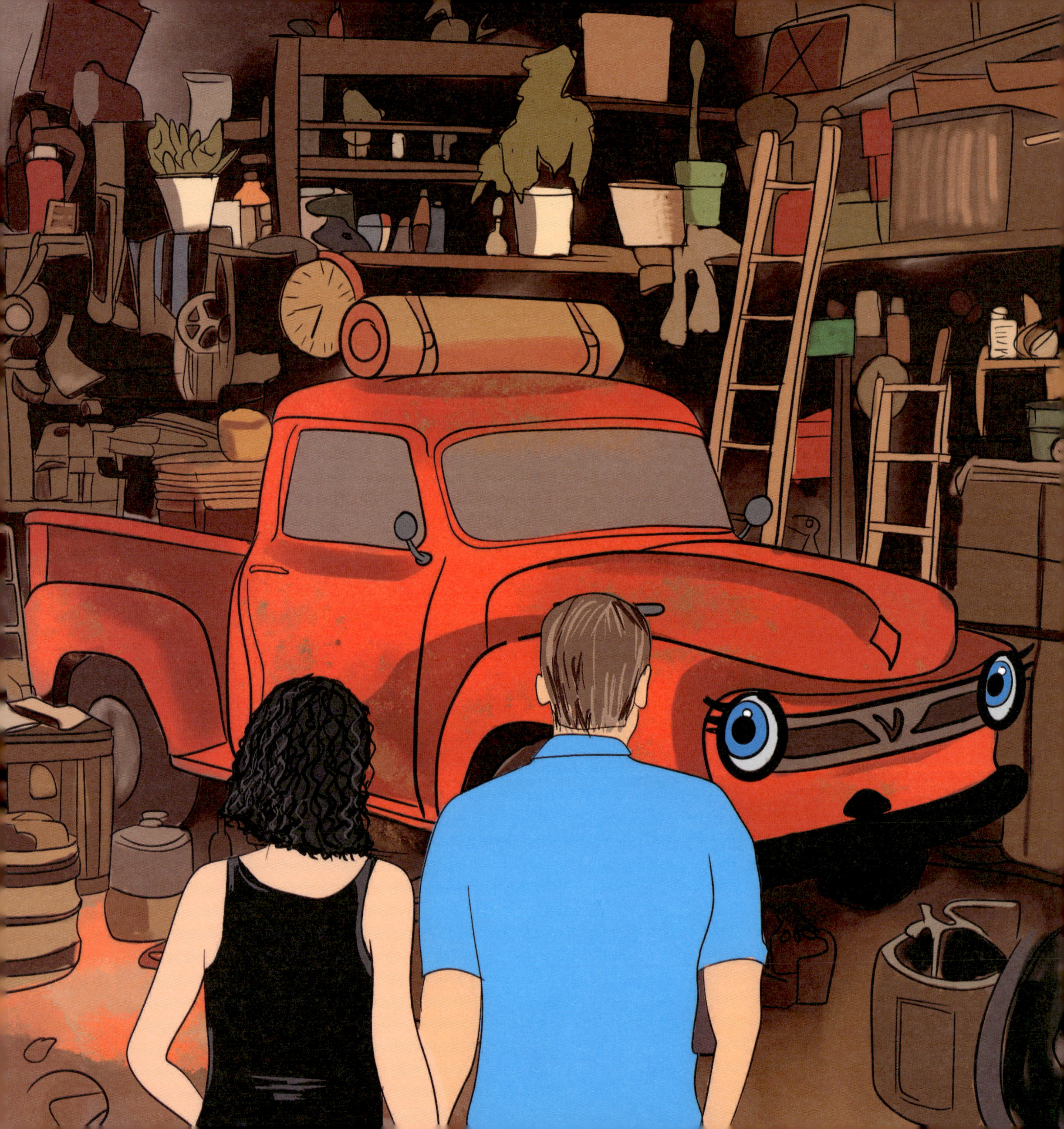

Rosie & Friends
Adventures of a FLOWER TRUCK

One sunny spring morning the garage door slowly opened and cool, fresh air rushed in. To the old truck's surprise there were two people she had never seen before standing alongside her owner. She wasn't sure why they were there but they got very excited when they saw her. There were comments from the visiting man and woman about what a "pretty girl" she was and how much they liked her. The man and his wife walked back and forth around her, even touching her front hood. Opening her door, sitting inside and looking under her hood, the new people were very excited about the truck and all of her features. No one ever talked to her like that before or gave her so much attention. It filled her with happiness.

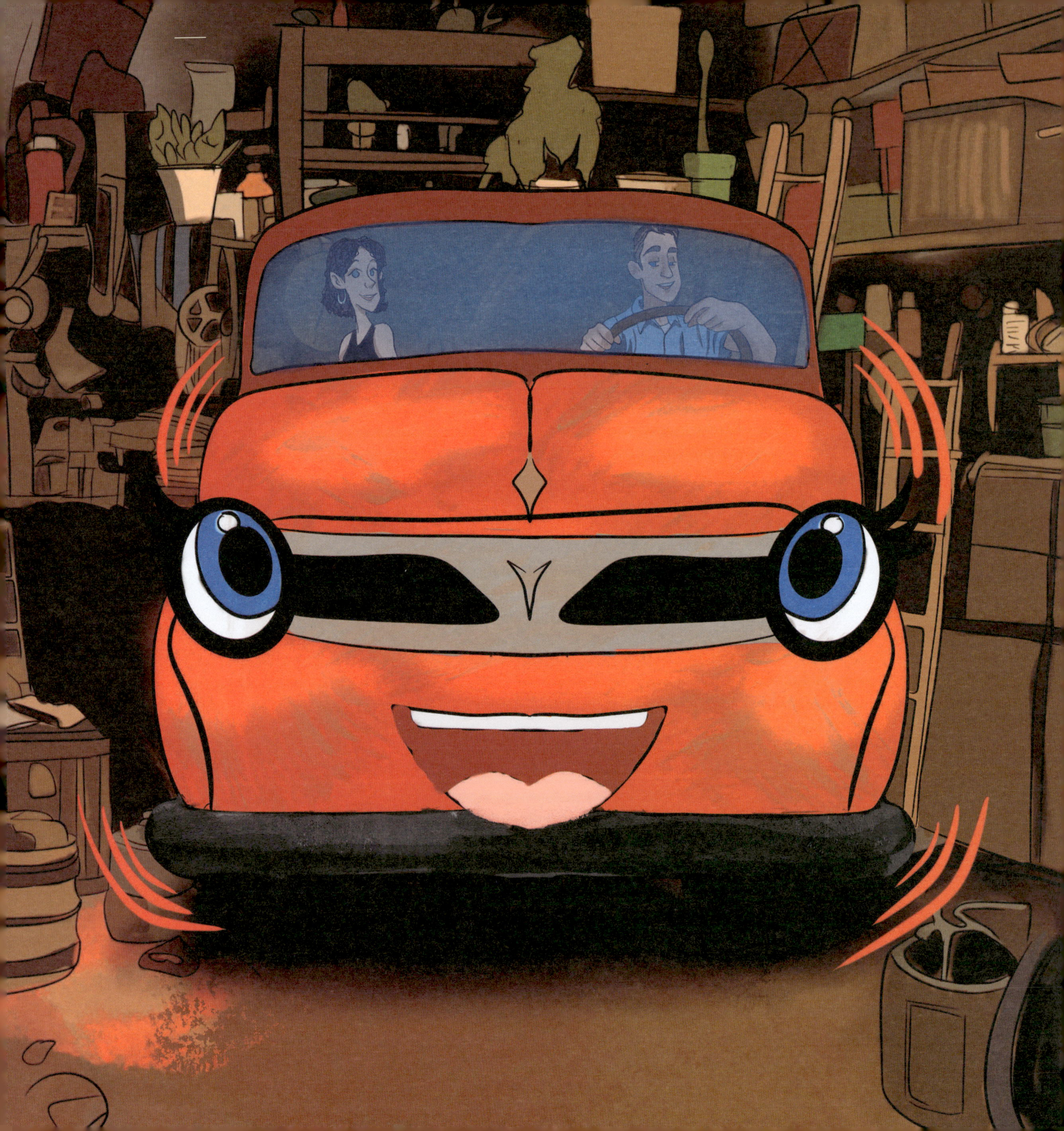

Rosie & Friends
Adventures of a FLOWER TRUCK

I hope they start my engine so I can really show them who I am, she thought, hoping they would turn the key in her ignition. And they did! The truck made sure she gave them her best motor sound,

VROOM! VROOM!

nice and loud. The old truck was very proud of herself, especially of how strong she was. The two people smiled and said such nice things about her, like, "Wow! Listen to that strong engine!"

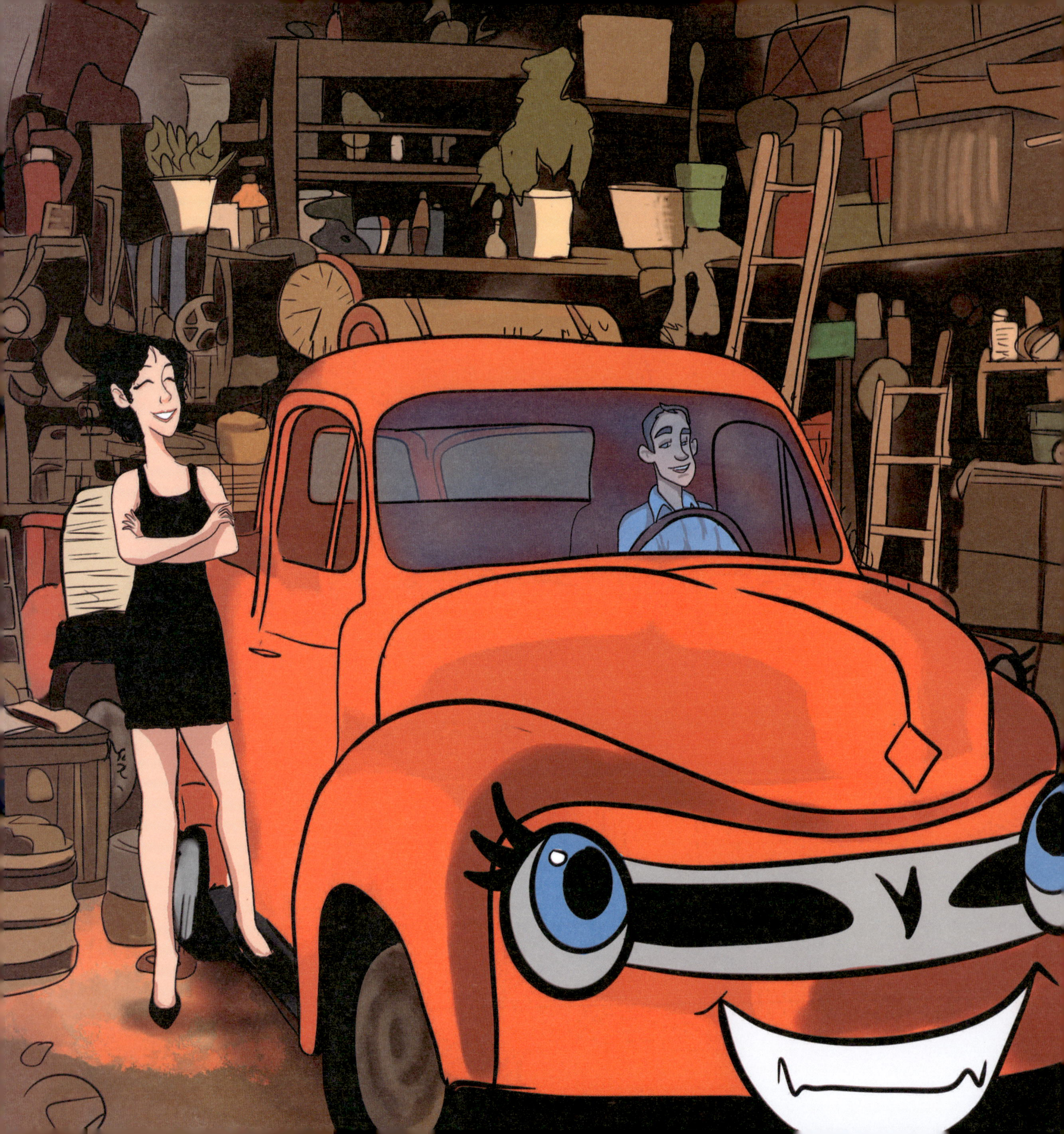

Rosie & Friends
Adventures of a FLOWER TRUCK

She was very proud to show off a little, even though she didn't know why they were visiting her in her garage home. Then she heard the best news ever . . . they were taking her with them and giving her a new home! She beeped her horn with joy, just once and not too loud, just to show how excited she was.

BEEP!

What will my new home be like? the truck wondered. *Will my wheels travel on roads again so I can see the countryside? Oh, I am so happy!*

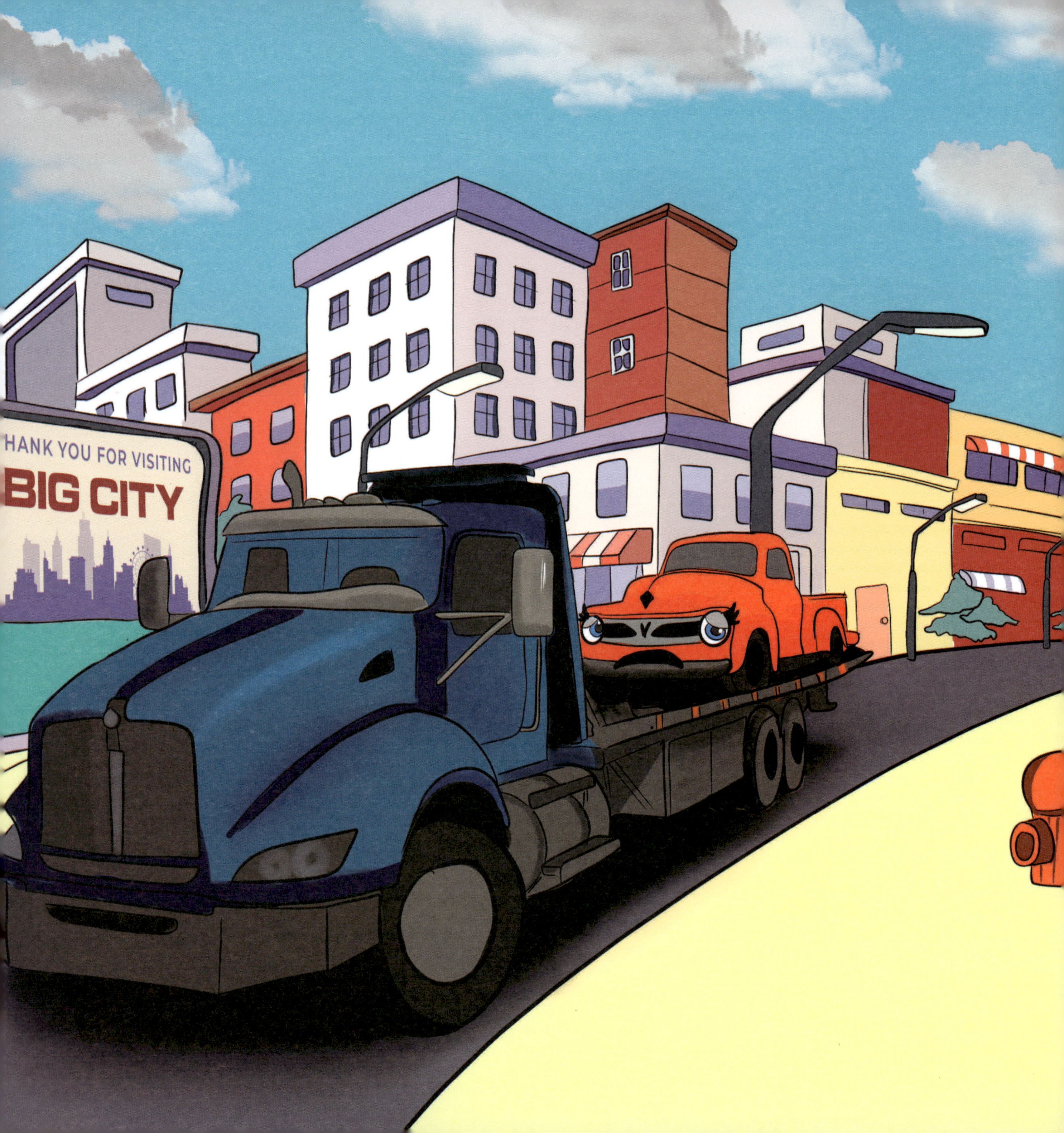
HANK YOU FOR VISITING
BIG CITY

Rosie & Friends
Adventures of a FLOWER TRUCK

The drive to her new home on the transport truck seemed to take forever but the old truck enjoyed being outside once again. She was so happy to be out of that dusty garage and starting a new life. Her trip included a drive through a crowded city with tall buildings with shiny windows. In the city, the cars crowded very close on either side… *It's way too crowded on these city roads,* she thought.

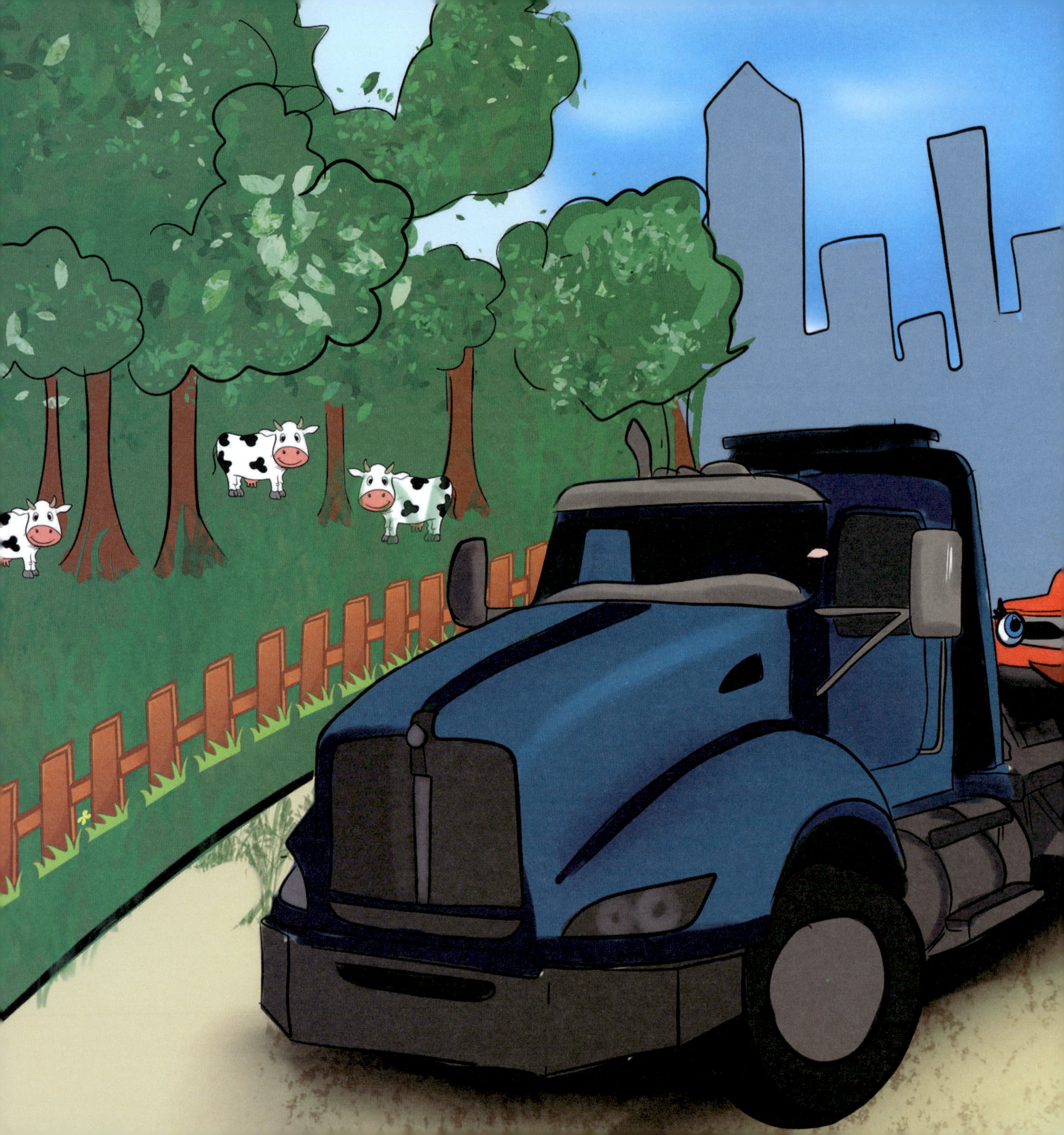

Rosie & Friends
Adventures of a FLOWER TRUCK

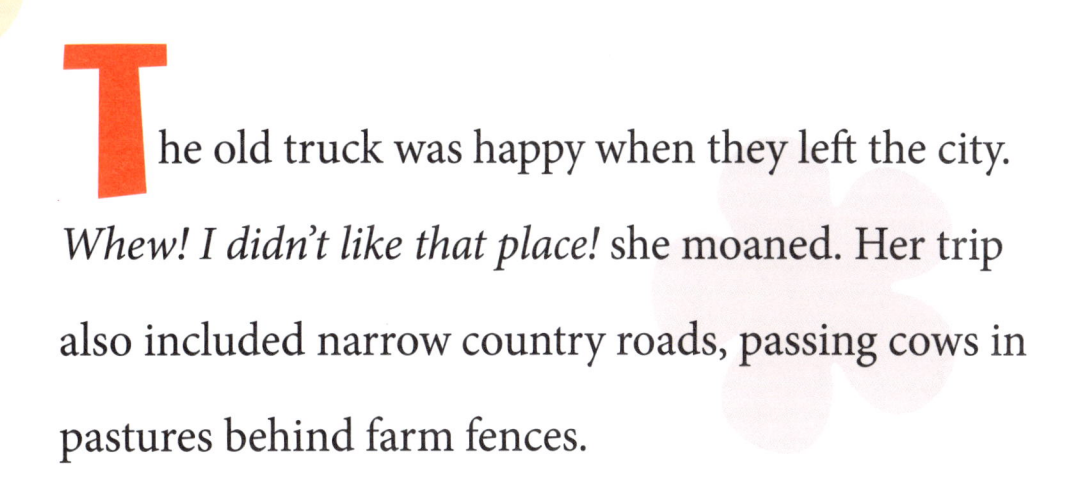

The old truck was happy when they left the city. *Whew! I didn't like that place!* she moaned. Her trip also included narrow country roads, passing cows in pastures behind farm fences.

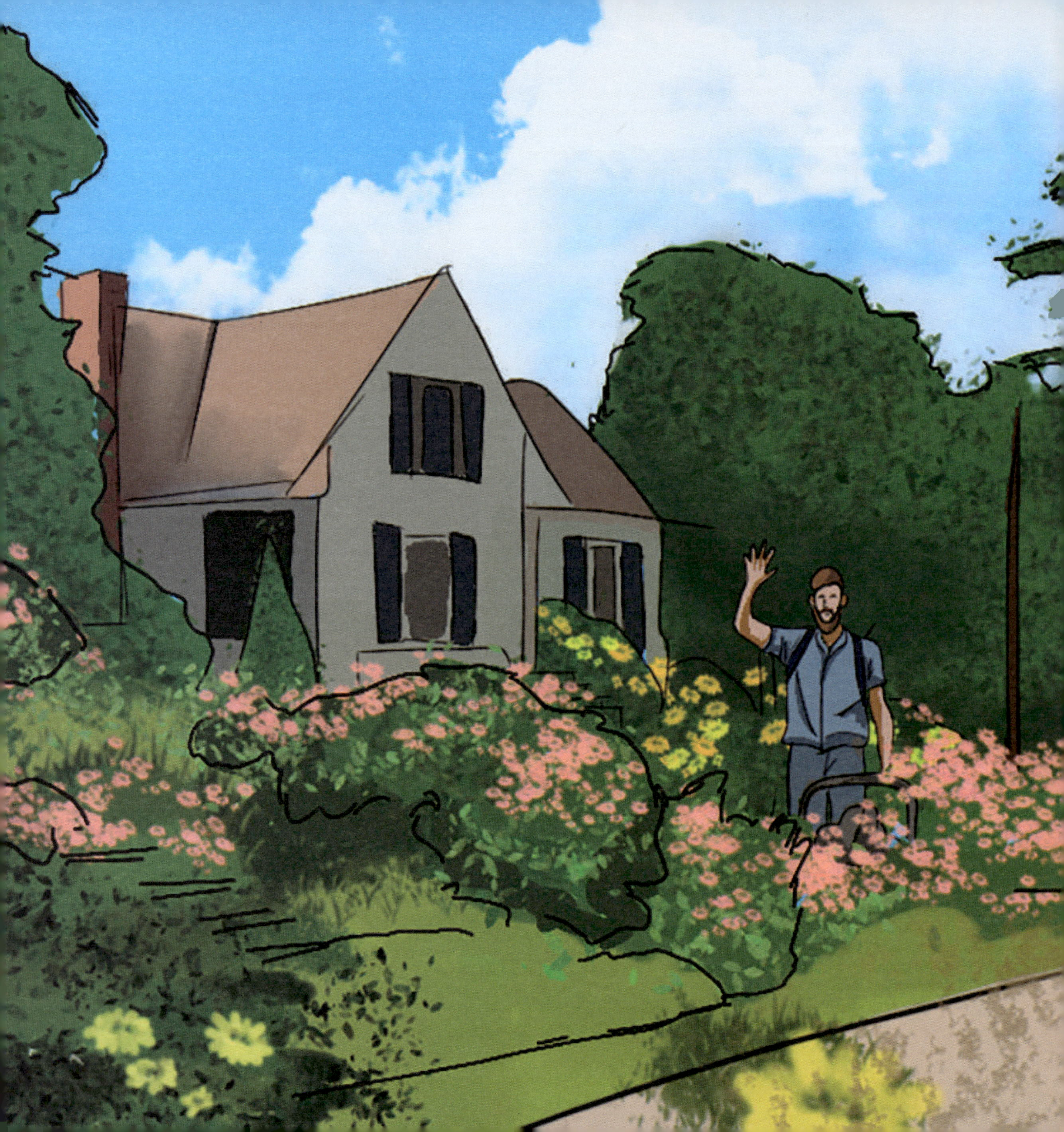

Rosie & Friends
Adventures of a FLOWER TRUCK

They entered a small town with family homes on both sides of the street. Friendly people worked in their yards planting flowers and waving to her new owners. *Ahh, this is so nice,* sighed the old truck.

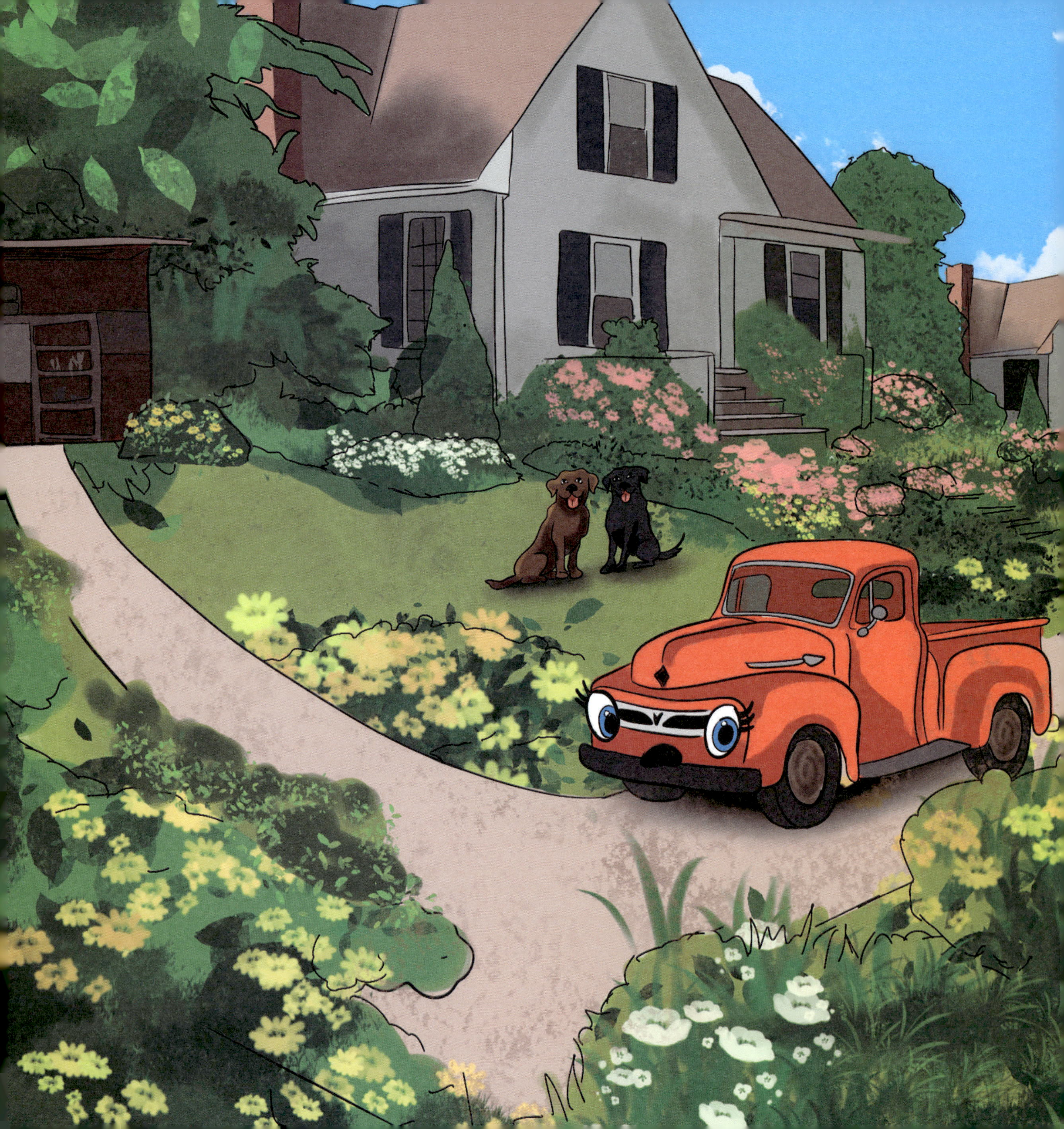

Rosie & Friends
Adventures of a FLOWER TRUCK

She was so busy watching the people that it surprised her when the transport truck pulled into a driveway and they unloaded her in front of a beautiful home with nice green grass and colorful spring flowers. It was lovely! *Was this her new home?* Oh, she hoped so! She found out very soon that it was.

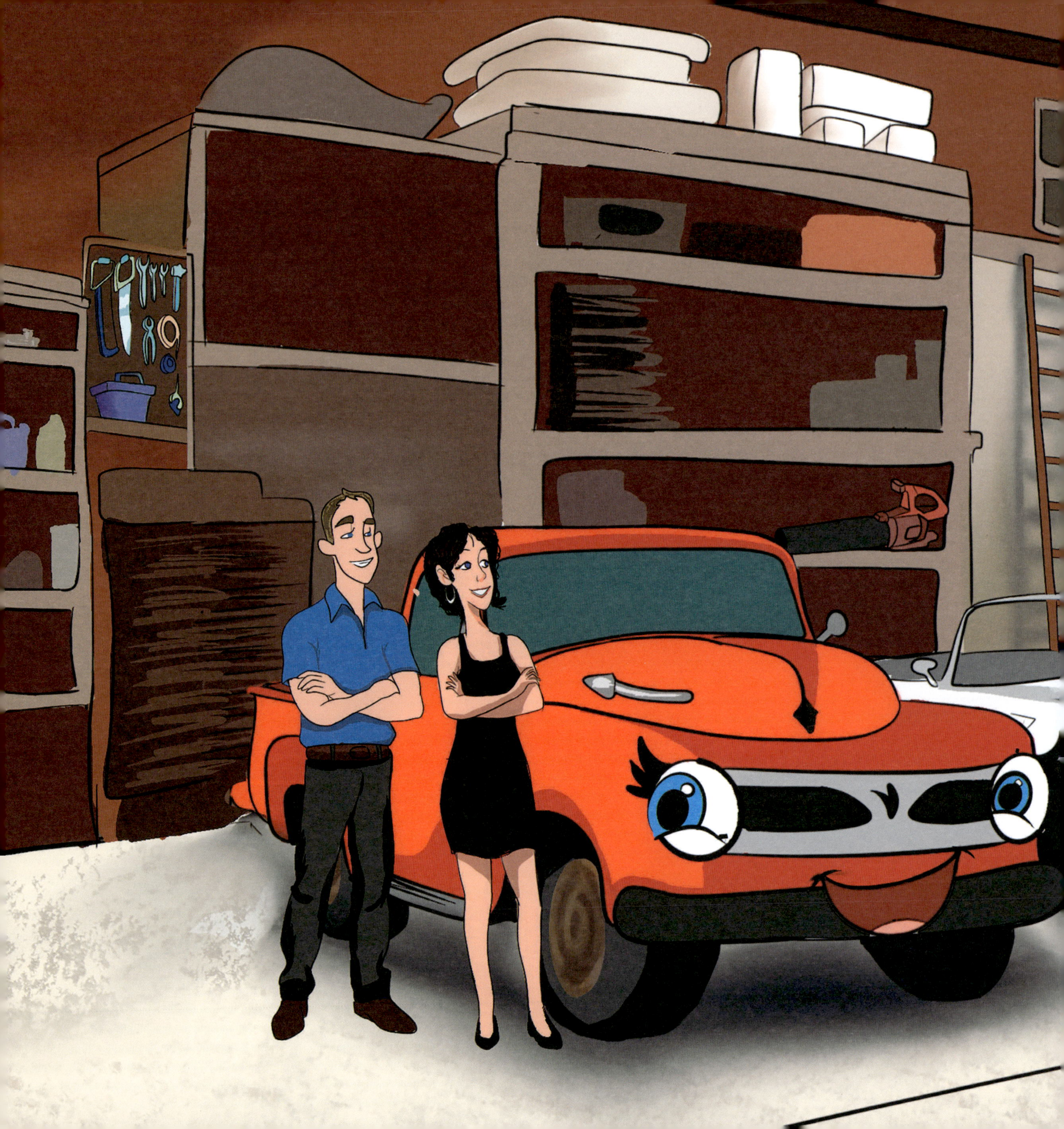

Rosie & Friends
Adventures of a FLOWER TRUCK

The garage was so BIG and CLEAN and had bright lights overhead. It even smelled clean, like fresh pine trees. Against the walls were a ladder and lots of tools on the shelves. Best of all, next to her was another car! Before she could introduce herself the woman laughed and said to the man, "Let's call her Rosie. Welcome home, Rosie!" The old red truck smiled. *Rosie! Wow! I have a name! I'm Rosie the red truck!* She could hardly believe it! A new home, a new name, a new family! Rosie couldn't remember being so happy. She had often dreamed of a new home like this, and now that dream had come true.

The man and woman smiled at her one more time, turned off the garage lights and left, but since it was still daylight, Rosie could look around her new home and discover even more.

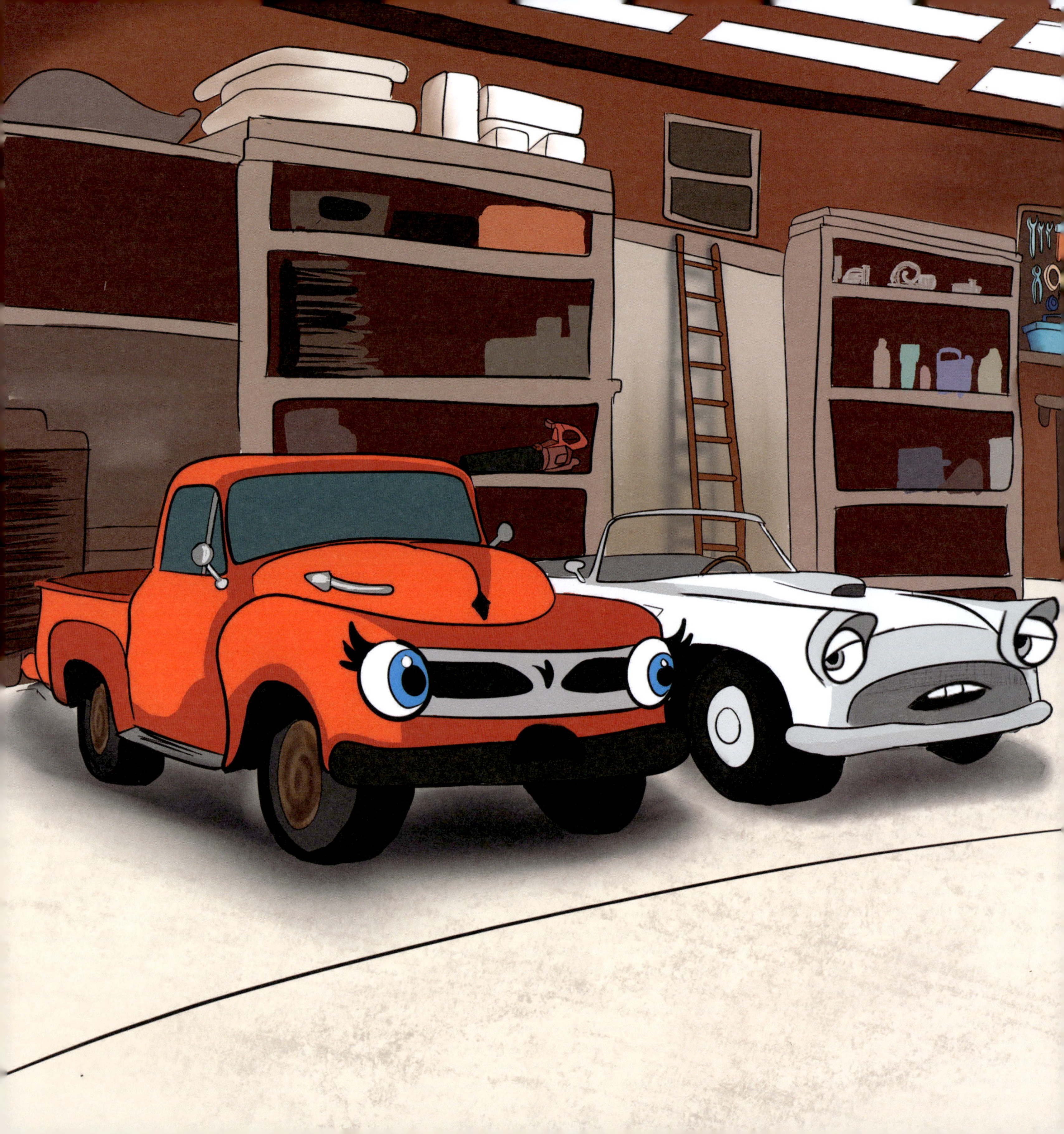

Rosie & Friends
Adventures of a Flower Truck

Rosie looked over at the car. It was a beautiful old shiny white auto. and she was surprised that it didn't have a top. Rosie thought it was the coolest thing ever! The tires were so clean and the white paint sparkled like glitter.

"Hi, I'm Eddie. What's your name?" the white car asked. Eddie's voice was very low and scratchy. It was soothing and it made Rosie smile.

"Hi, I'm Rosie." She beamed with pleasure as she said her new name.

"You'll love it here. The family takes good care of me and I'm sure they'll love you just as they love me," Eddie told her. Rosie couldn't wait!

"Why don't you have a roof over your seats?" Rosie asked.

"I'm a convertible, which means I can take my roof off sometimes," Eddie explained.

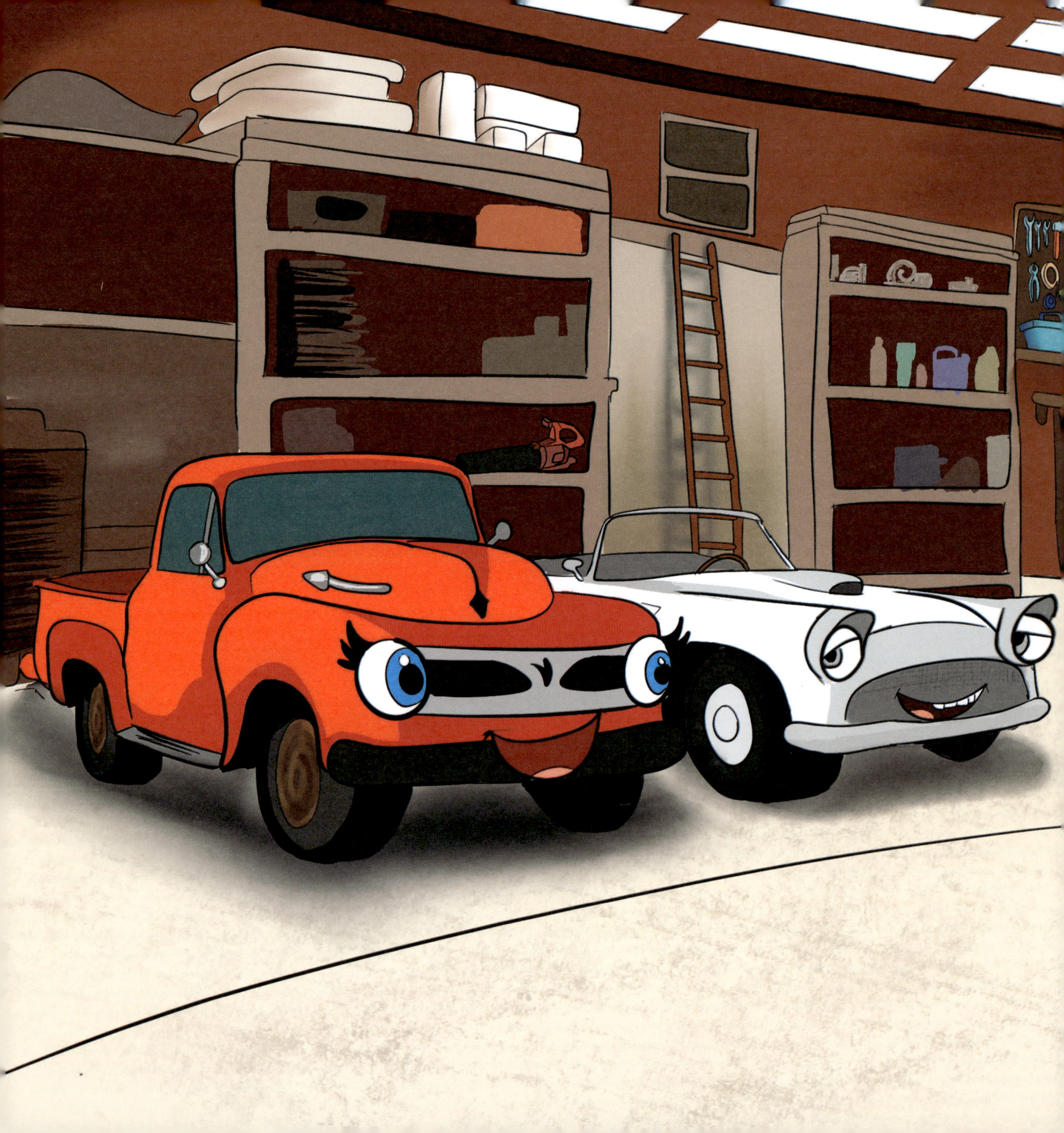

Rosie & Friends
Adventures of a FLOWER TRUCK

"WOW! That is just so cool!" Rosie said with excitement. She noticed that Eddie also had shiny silver bumpers and white wheels. She thought Eddie was so handsome and she hoped one day to be just as pretty, but in her own special way.

The next few days in her new garage home were filled with excitement . . . under the truck, inside the truck, under the hood, up, down, inside and out, every part of Rosie was checked out to the fullest. And after all of that work, *she was so tired*.

She couldn't remember the last time she had so much attention and work done to her. She was fitted with four new tires, bigger and prettier than the old ones, like new shoes that make you run faster and jump higher.

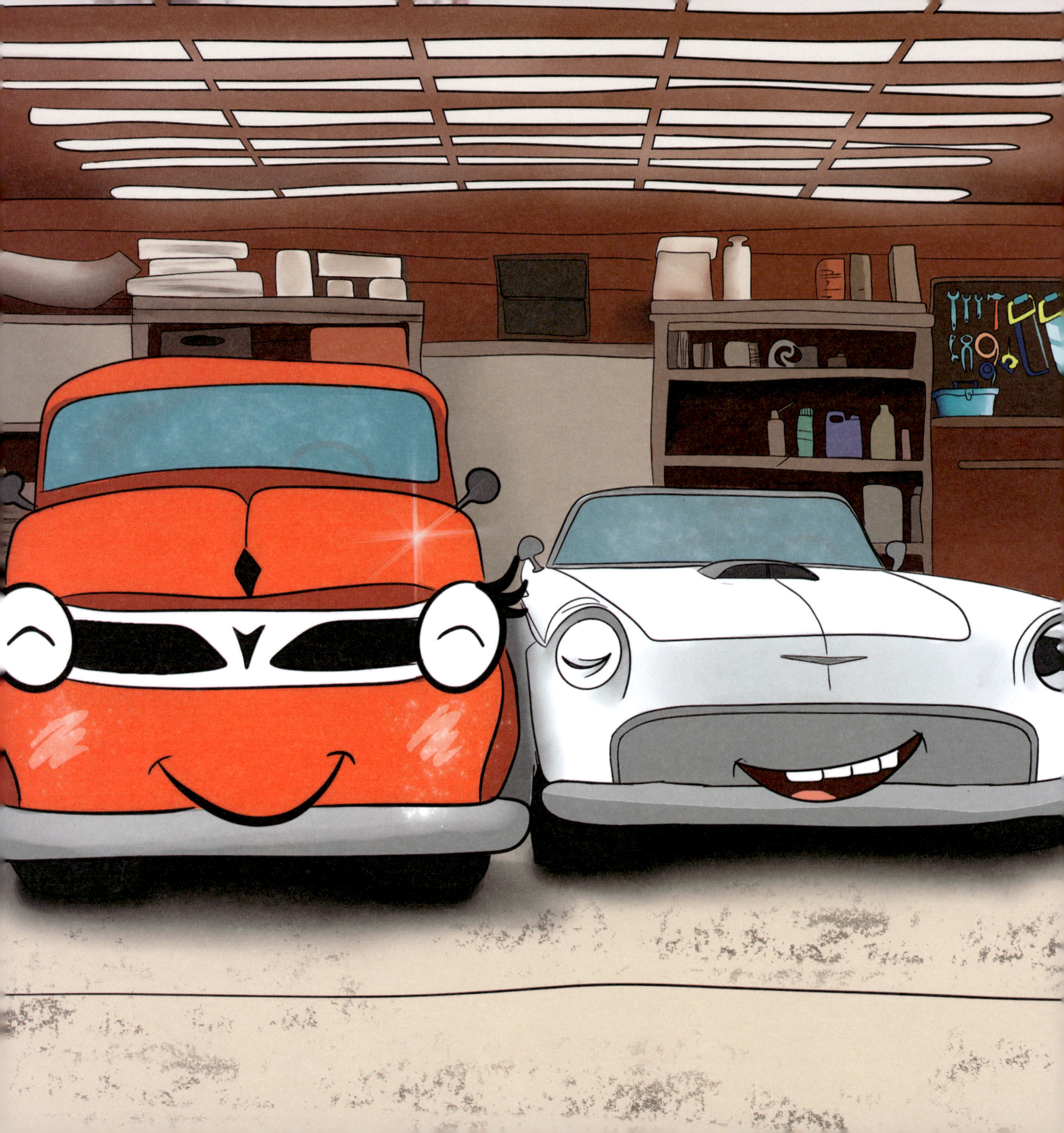

Rosie & Friends
Adventures of a FLOWER TRUCK

New oil was poured into her engine to be sure she could drive smoothly. It was silky and smooth and made her feel young again. *I bet I can really drive fast now,* she thought. Her horn even got a tune up so it was nice and loud.

BEEP! BEEP!

Wow! I can't wait to go out on the roads and beep HELLO to all my new neighbors! she thought. But her favorite part of the all the new changes were the shiny new chrome bumpers. Her dull, dirty, old rusty ones were now shiny and new, front and back, *just like Eddie's!* Rosie felt very special now. She couldn't wait to leave the garage to show off her new look.

"You look beautiful!" Eddie winked at her when the work on Rosie was all done. Rosie, the old red truck, beamed with excitement. She was the happiest she had ever been! What new adventures were ahead?

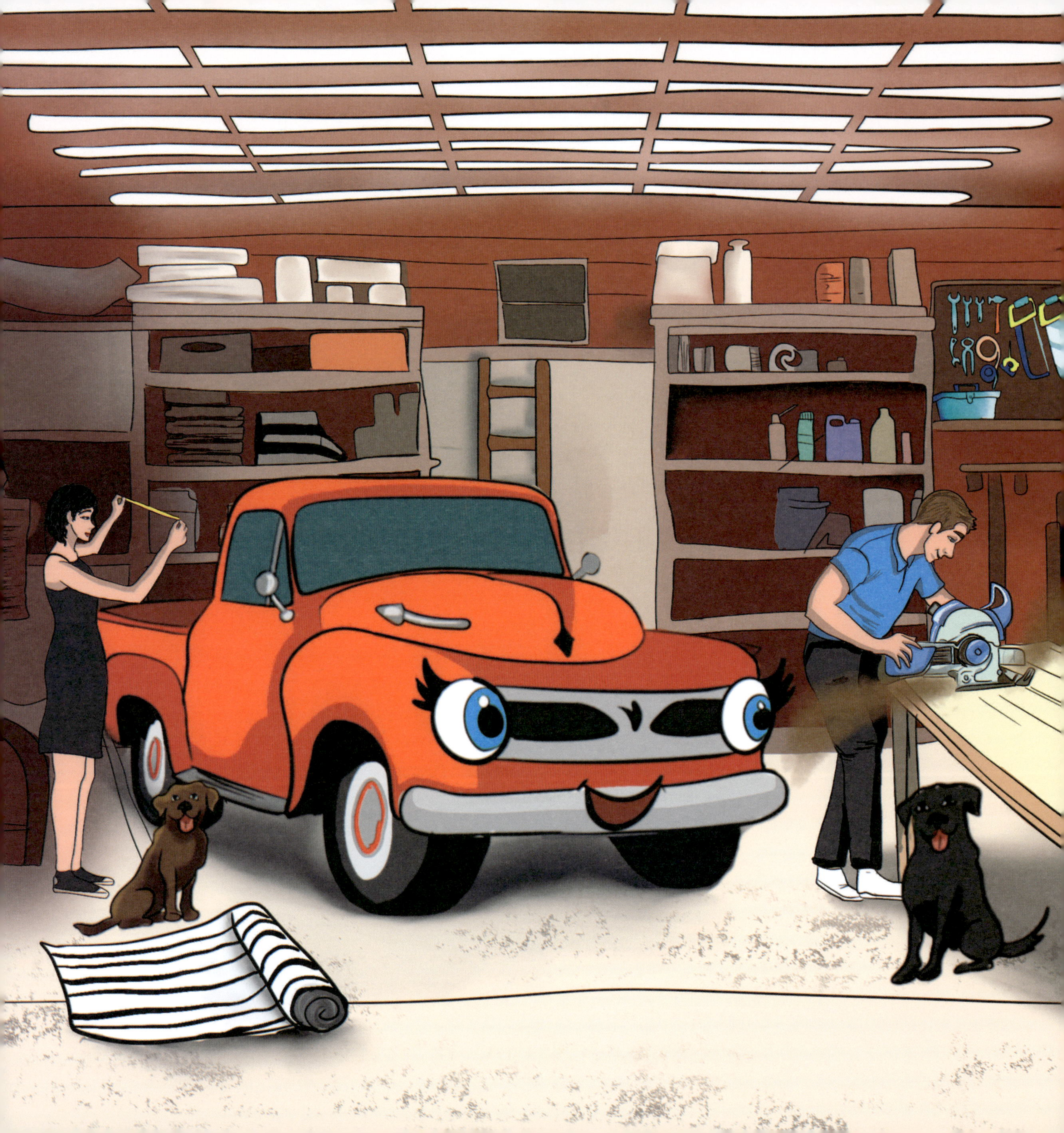

Rosie & Friends
Adventures of a FLOWER TRUCK

The next day, something strange started happening. There was lots of noise in the garage, banging and drilling and sawing.

BANG! BANG! BZZZZZZ!

The man was cutting wood into all different sizes and screwing them together. Dust flew in every direction. The woman kept measuring the back of Rosie and then going to the sewing machine and sewing lots of fabric. All day her new family worked around Rosie in the garage and before she knew it *Rosie had a brand new look!*

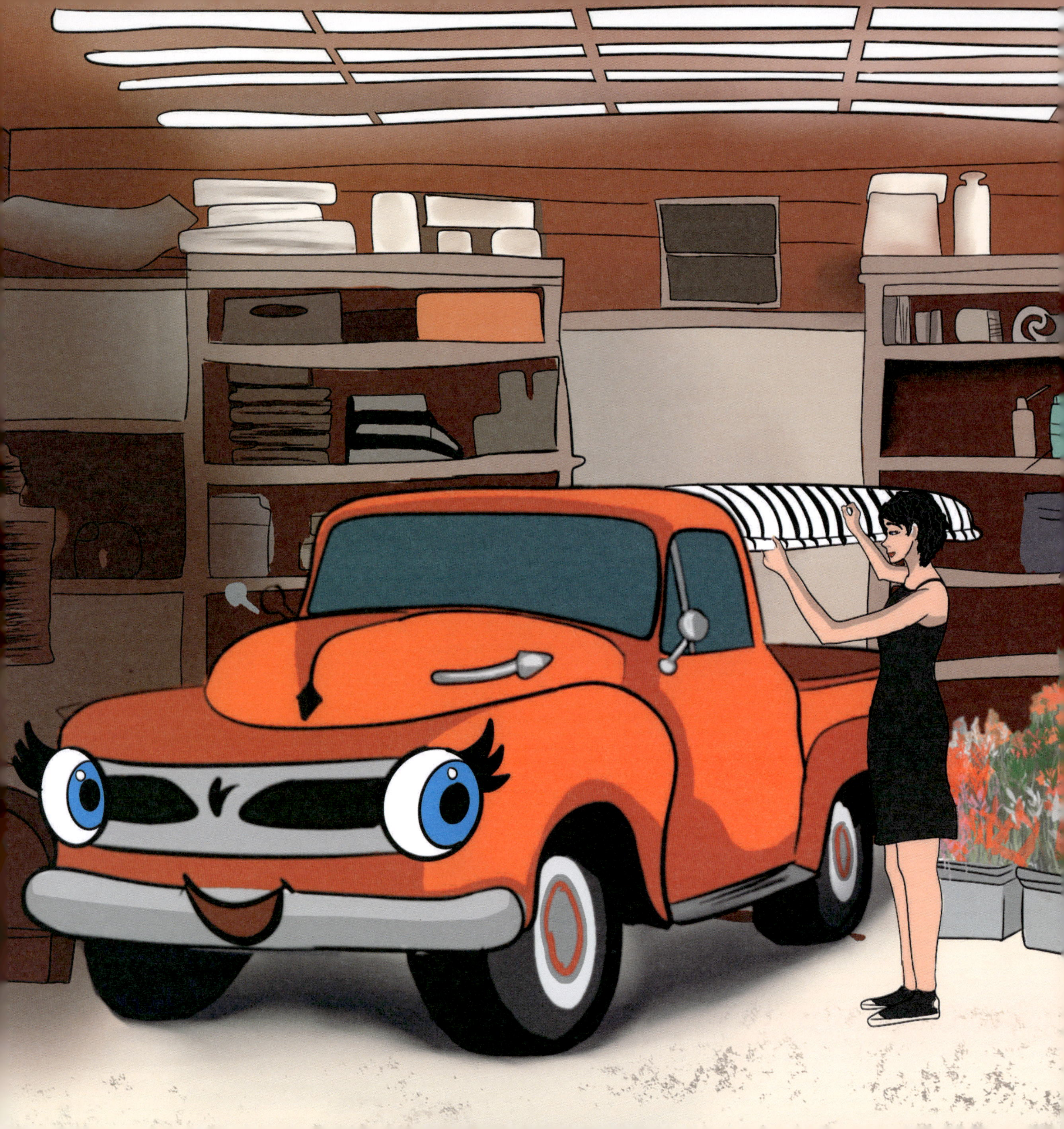

Rosie & Friends
Adventures of a FLOWER TRUCK

She had a large wooden frame on her back, covered with a beautiful white-and-black striped canopy, and lots of silver buckets would be placed in her truck bed. Eddie had never seen anything like it! Rosie had no idea what was going on. It was all new to her, too. *What could be happening?* Rosie wondered. She was a bit worried. New things always seem scary in the beginning.

Then something magical happened! The man and woman filled the silver buckets with beautiful flowers, every color and shape Rosie could imagine, tall flowers, short flowers, skinny flowers, and fat flowers. Rosie was transformed into something so special she thought she would burst her hubcaps with joy.

Eddie couldn't believe his eyes. "Rosie, you're a FLOWER TRUCK!!" he exclaimed when all the work was done. Rosie was also excited, even though she didn't know what a flower truck was.

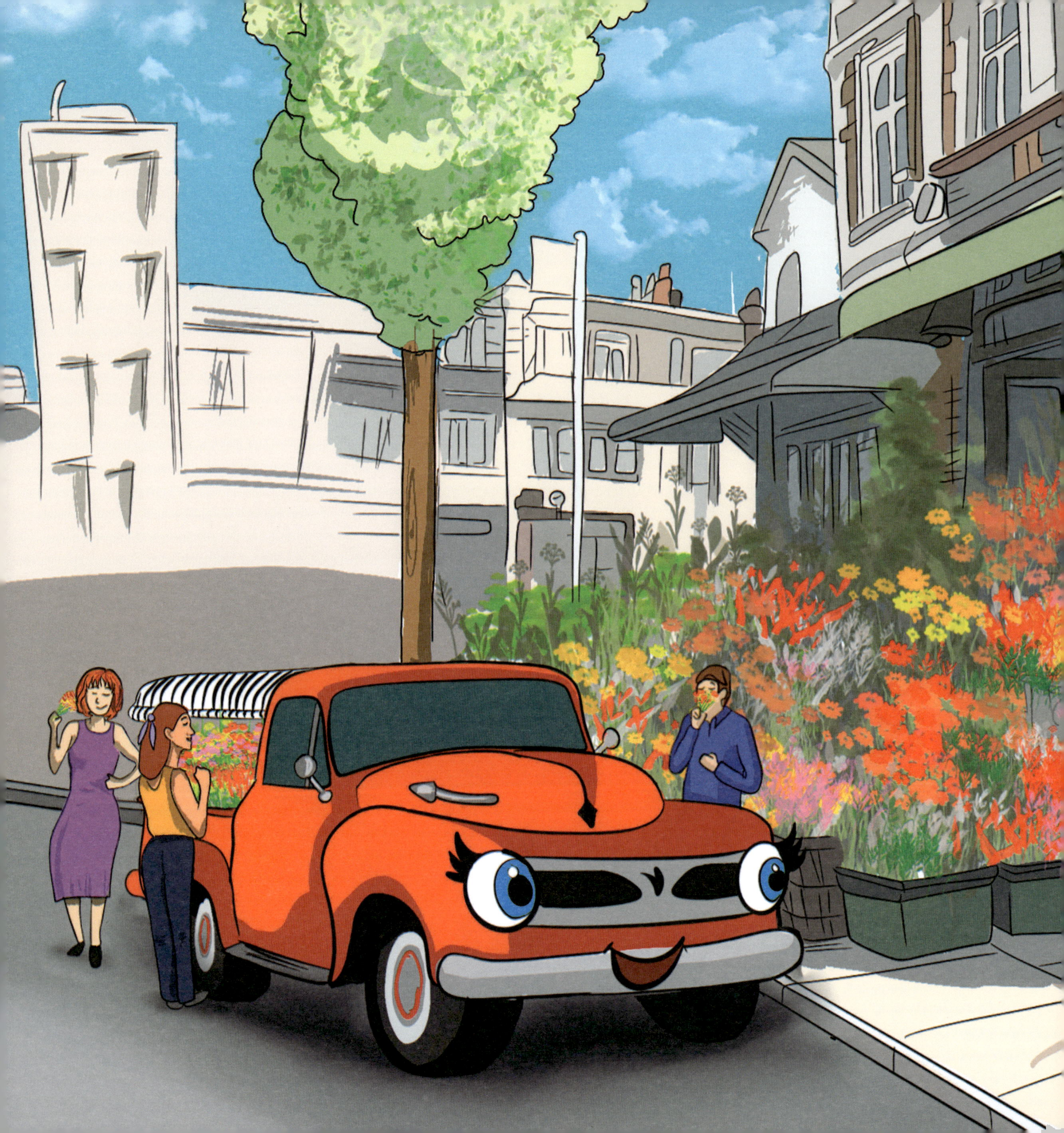

Rosie & Friends
Adventures of a Flower Truck

"What does it mean to be a flower truck, Eddie?"

"I don't know," Eddie replied softly. "but you are filled with bunches and bunches of beautiful, colorful flowers." So many flowers! Round yellow ones, pink ones that looked like stars, orange and purple ones. They were all so pretty and smelled so good! Rosie felt like she was ready to change the world!

Soon, Rosie was out of the garage and on the road almost every day, filled with all of those beautiful flowers. She visited schools and stores and businesses and libraries. People would walk around her in wonder while picking out beautiful flowers to buy. They would smile and sigh and smell the flowers.

SNIFF. SNIFF.

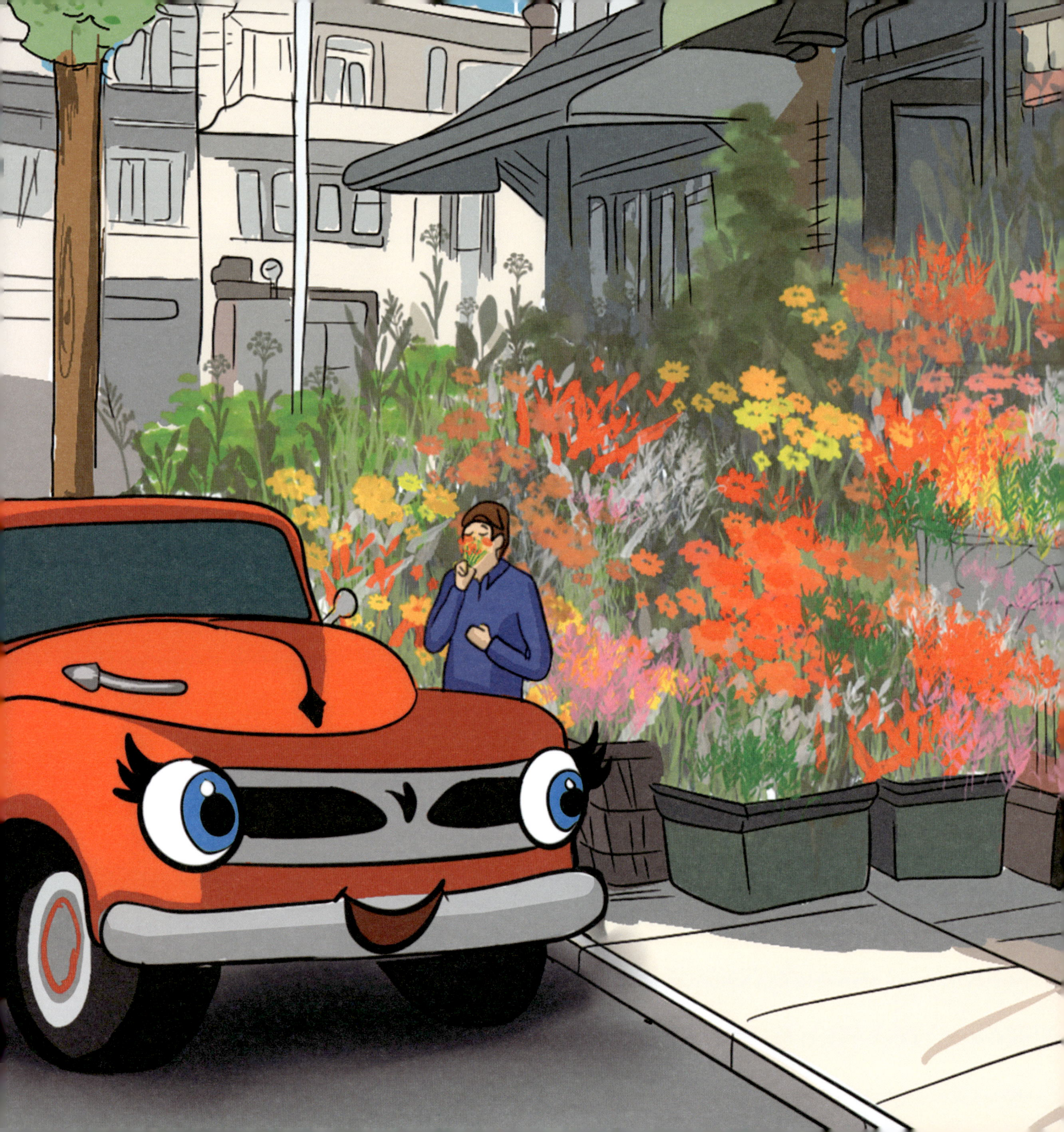

Rosie & Friends
Adventures of a FLOWER TRUCK

They all seemed so happy to be with Rosie and her truckload of happy flowers—yellow sunflowers, orange poppies, purple roses, pink lilies, and white daisies. Rosie felt so different when she was filled with those fun and fancy flowers. Now that she had a real purpose she felt happy and useful, just like she had always dreamed of feeling.

"My wife will love these flowers!" one man said, picking out an entire bouquet one by one by one.

"I can't wait to give these flowers to my mom!" said a smiling young man.

"These flowers will look fantastic on my dining room table!" an older woman said softly.

Rosie realized that making others happy made her happy, too. It was a wonderful feeling that she hoped would continue forever, every season, every year. It was such a good lesson that she made sure she kept it in her heart every day.

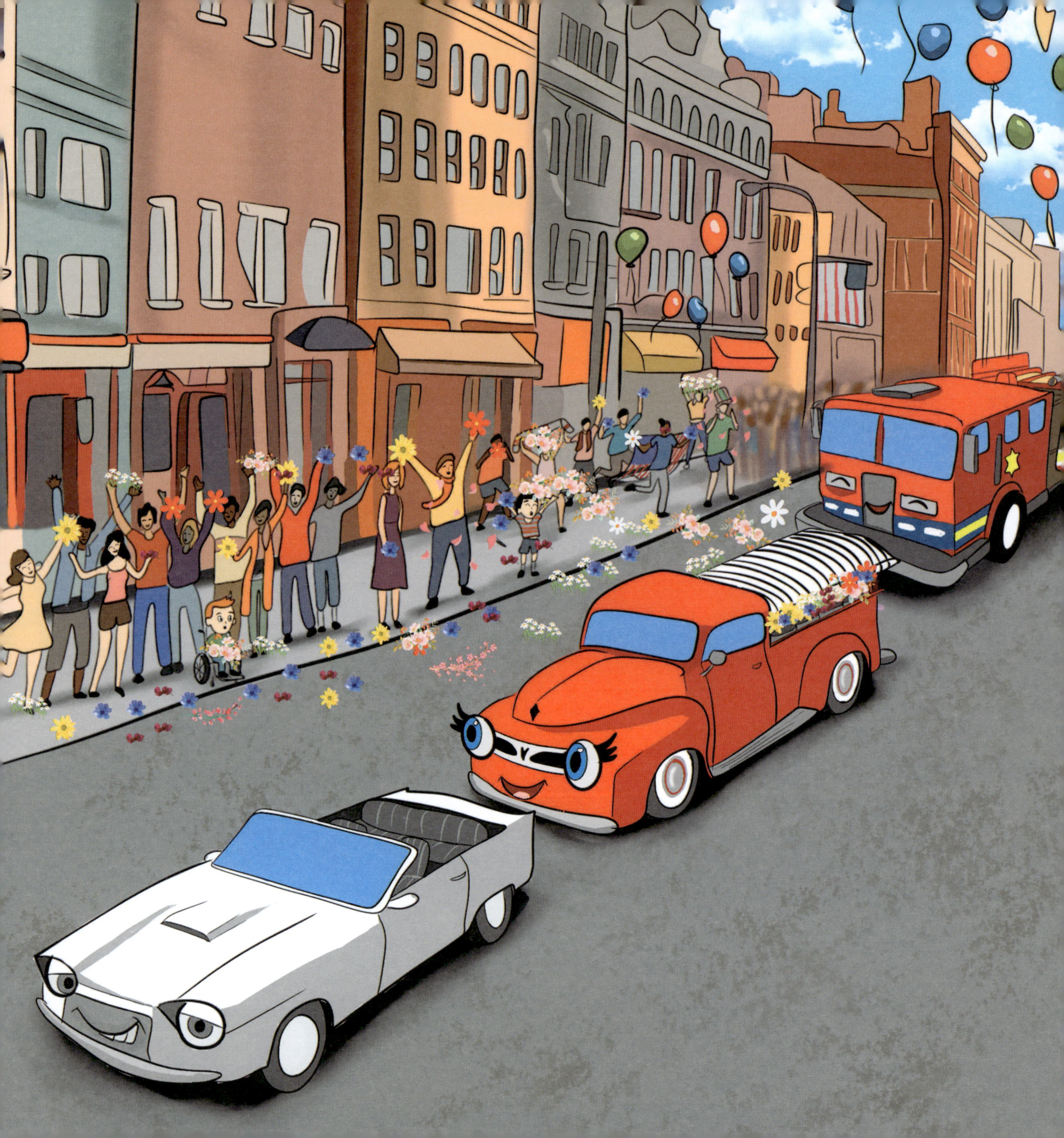

Rosie & Friends
Adventures of a FLOWER TRUCK

One of Rosie's favorite things to do was drive in parades. Crowds of people along both sides of the streets, families with their children and dogs, it was a noisy and fun sight to see street after street. As she drove by, Rosie beamed with excitement when the people waved and called her name, "Rosie, Rosie, throw us a flower!" Rosie would beep her horn

BEEP! BEEP!

and throw flowers to the folks along the streets.

She loved hearing the marching bands, the drums going

BOOM! BOOM! BOOM!

while the people clapped along. The big red firetrucks were always her favorite part. Rosie loved it when they beeped their big, deep horns and let loose those loud sirens.

Rosie & Friends
Adventures of a FLOWER TRUCK

Rosie made friends with Hank, the lead fire engine, and they would sound off their horns at each other in a friendly greeting,

HONK! HONK! from Hank and

BEEP! BEEP!

from Rosie. Sometimes Eddie would even join them. He would take his roof off and turn into a convertible. Eddie always looked so cool! He often winked at Rosie when they made a turn around the corner.

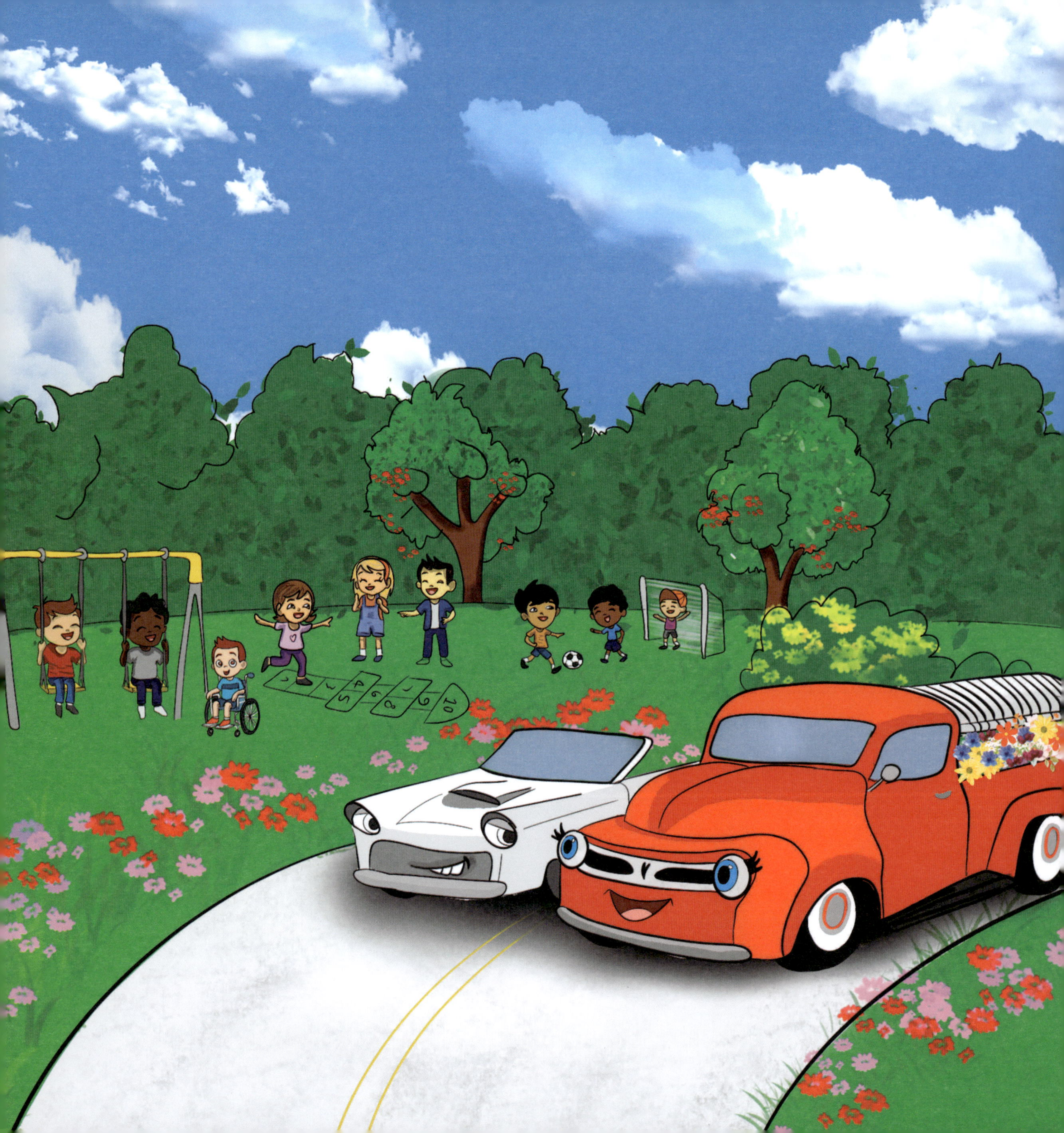

Rosie & Friends
Adventures of a FLOWER TRUCK

Just for fun, when Rosie wasn't working, she and Eddie would drive around together. They liked to drive past the cows in the pastures on those narrow winding country roads. Rosie and Eddie looked so beautiful that when others passed them they would often get beeps and thumbs up and waves. They liked to drive to the park to watch children swing on the swings, higher and higher, and slide down the slippery slides. Rosie and Eddie loved to watch the children laugh together.

HA! HA! HA!

Some children played hopscotch while others played soccer. It always looked like the children were having so much fun!

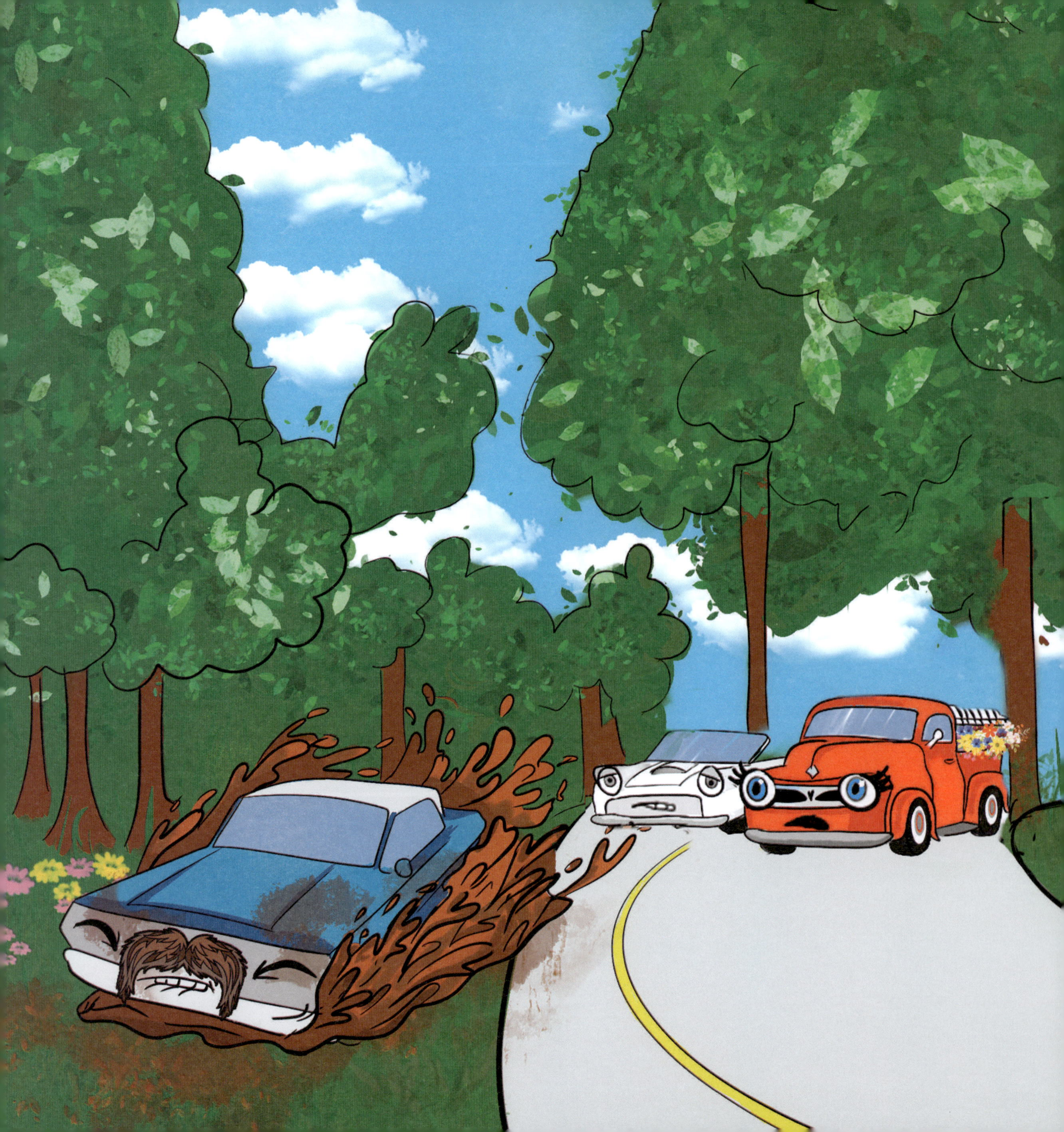

Rosie & Friends
Adventures of a FLOWER TRUCK

One day, while they were driving together on a narrow country road, they came across a handsome blue car with a white top. Rosie thought it was a bit odd that the car had a different colored roof. It was also older, like Eddie and Rosie. When they got closer they realized the old blue car was stuck in a deep puddle. He was covered in mud because his tires just kept spinning to get free and mud had flown all over the place in every direction, pushing him deeper and deeper into the puddle.

What a mess, thought Rosie.

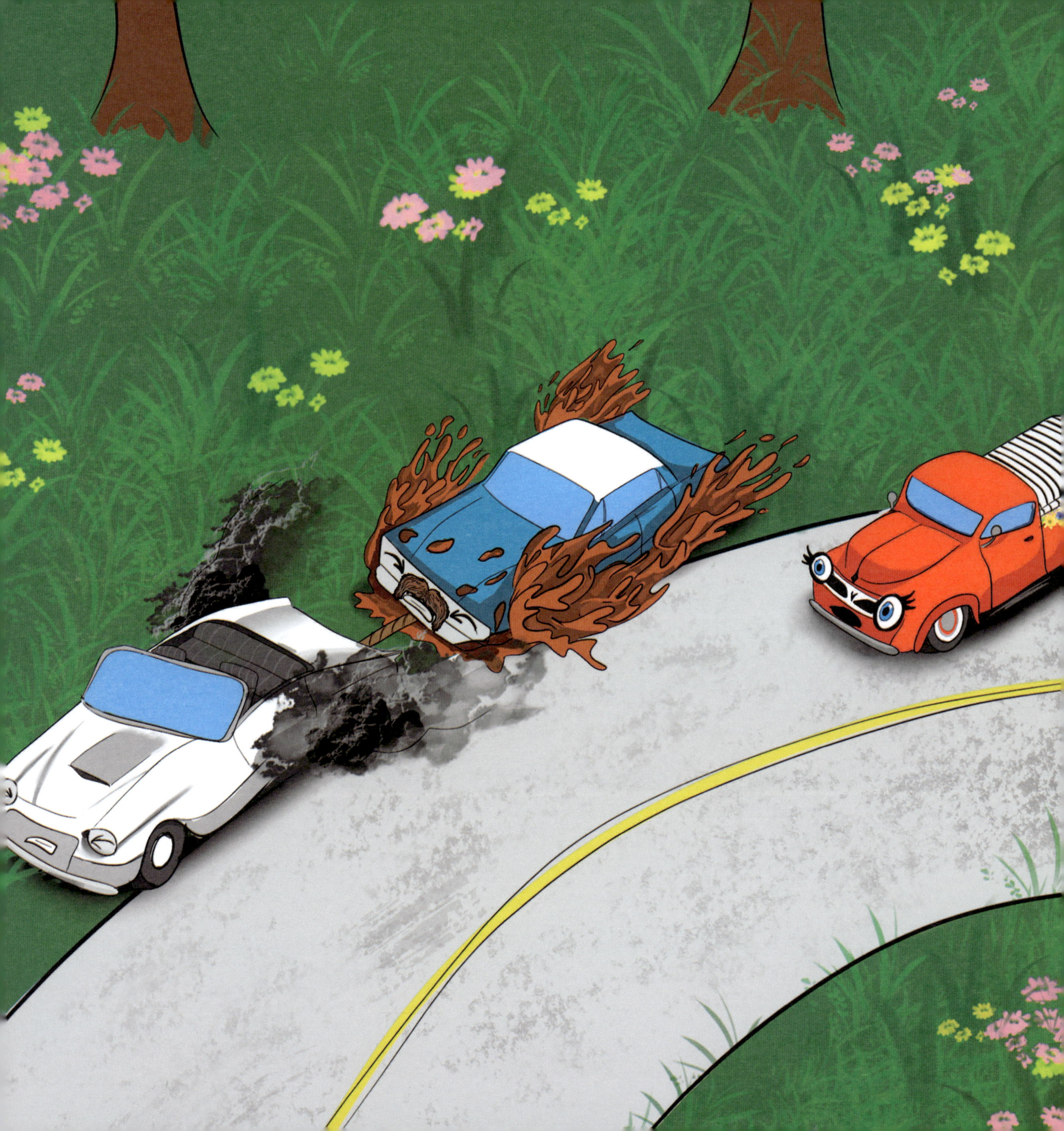

Rosie & Friends
Adventures of a FLOWER TRUCK

Eddie said, "Hi, I'm Eddie. Do you need help getting out of the mud?"

The blue car looked sad and said, "Yes, please. I've been trying to get out for a long time and I just can't move."

Eddie said, "I'll get you out in no time."

The blue car smiled. "I'm Dibo. Thank you so much!"

A rope was tied to the front of Dibo and to the back of Eddie. Rosie watched while Eddie tried pulling Dibo from the mud but he didn't move one inch. Eddie revved his engine

VVVVVROOM! VVVVVROOM!

and pulled with all his might but his tires just spun and spun until they started smoking. It wasn't working. Rosie stepped in and asked, "Can I try?"

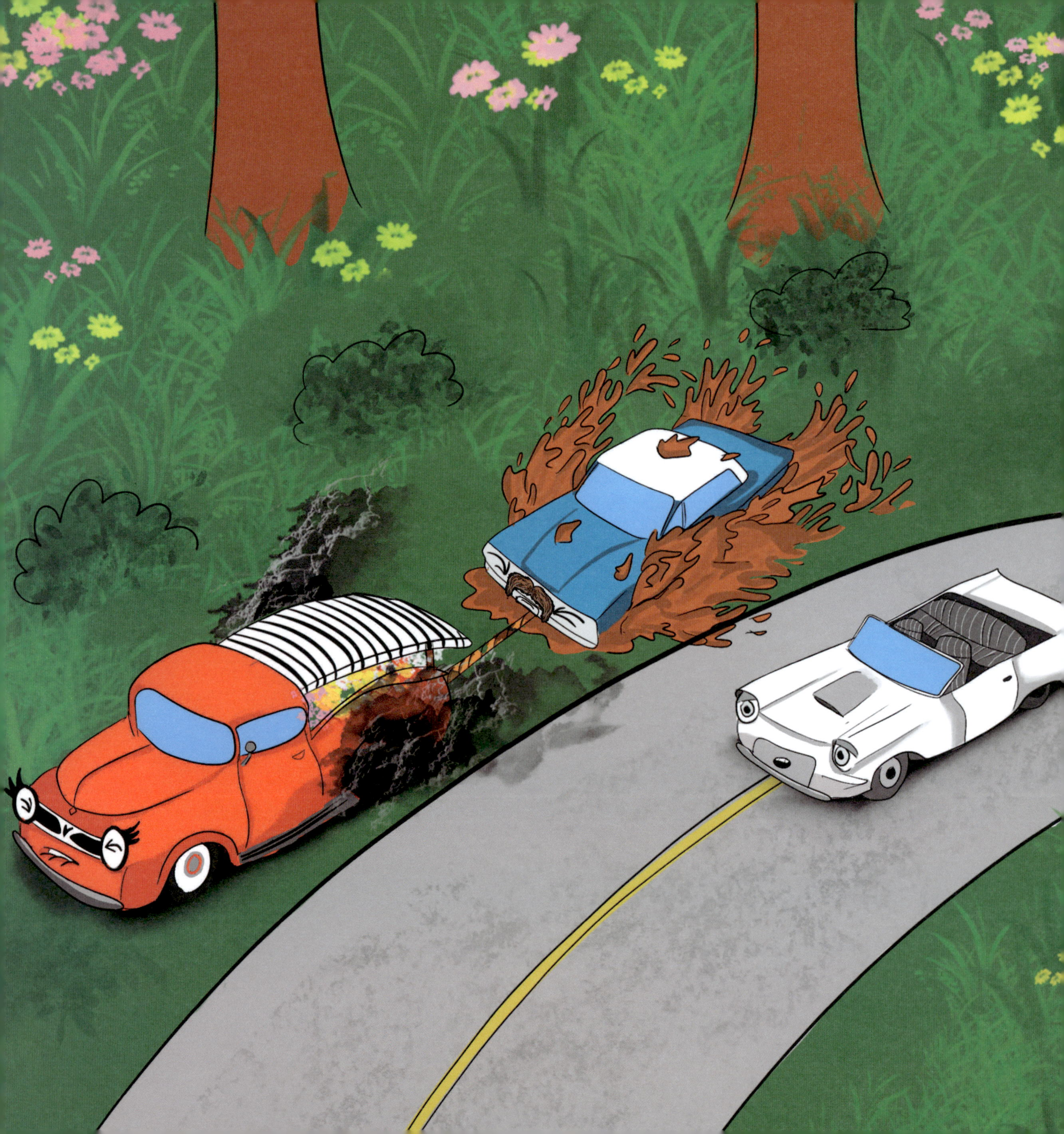

Rosie & Friends
Adventures of a FLOWER TRUCK

"I think we should call a tow truck," Eddie said sadly.

Rosie said, more strongly this time, "I'd like to try first." Eddie moved over and Rosie took over. Rosie pulled with all her strength.

GRRRR! GRRRR! VROOM!

In no time at all Rosie got Dibo out of the mud. The two boys were very surprised!

Dibo said, "Wow, you're strong . . . *for a girl*."

Rosie responded with a smile. "No. I'm just STRONG!" She knew that a girl could be strong and sometimes even stronger than a boy. Rosie loved being strong. She knew she could help people and she rarely needed others to help her. The boys agreed that Rosie was able to rescue Dibo because she was so strong, and they admired her for that.

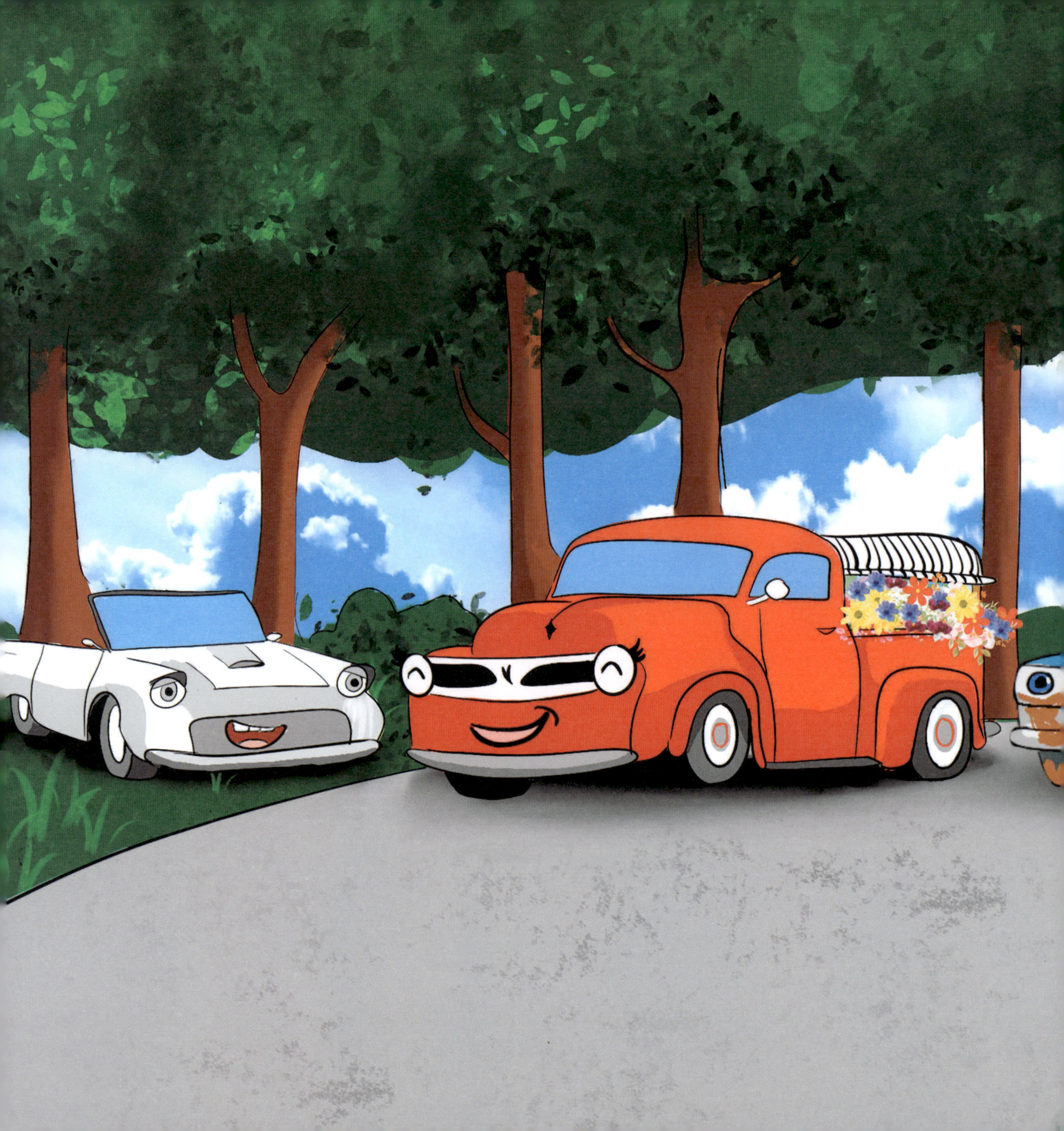

Rosie & Friends
Adventures of a FLOWER TRUCK

"Let's get you to a car wash. You're filthy," said Rosie.

"That's a great idea. I have so much mud on me I can hardly see!" Dibo admitted.

The three of them drove off together to find a car wash and get their new blue friend cleaned up and looking handsome again.

SWISH! SWISH!

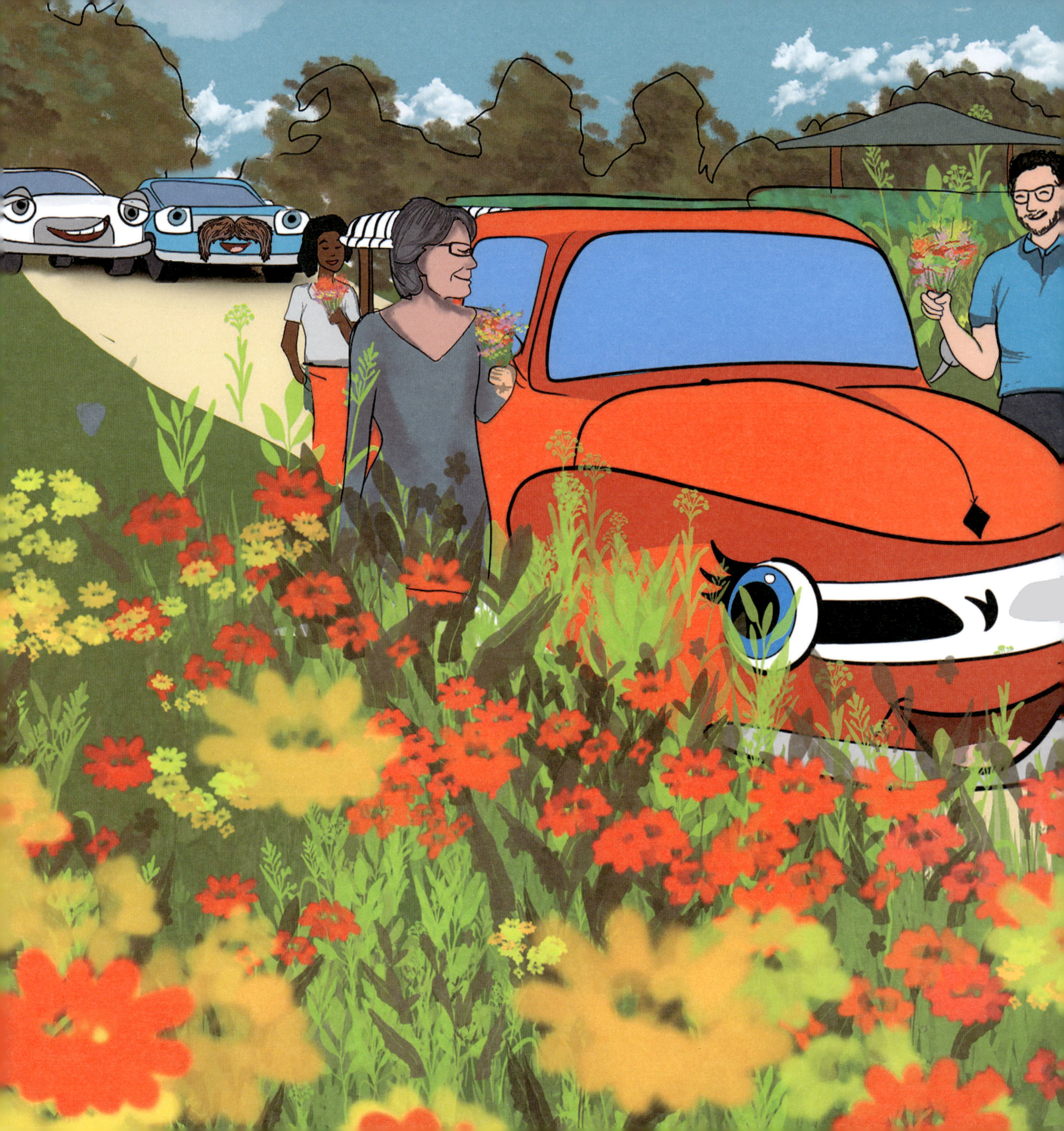

Rosie & Friends
Adventures of a FLOWER TRUCK

After this mess in the mud the three of them became best friends. Eddie and Dibo would travel with Rosie to her flower events to keep her company. They would watch in amazement at how much joy the flowers would bring as people walked around Rosie to select each special flower.

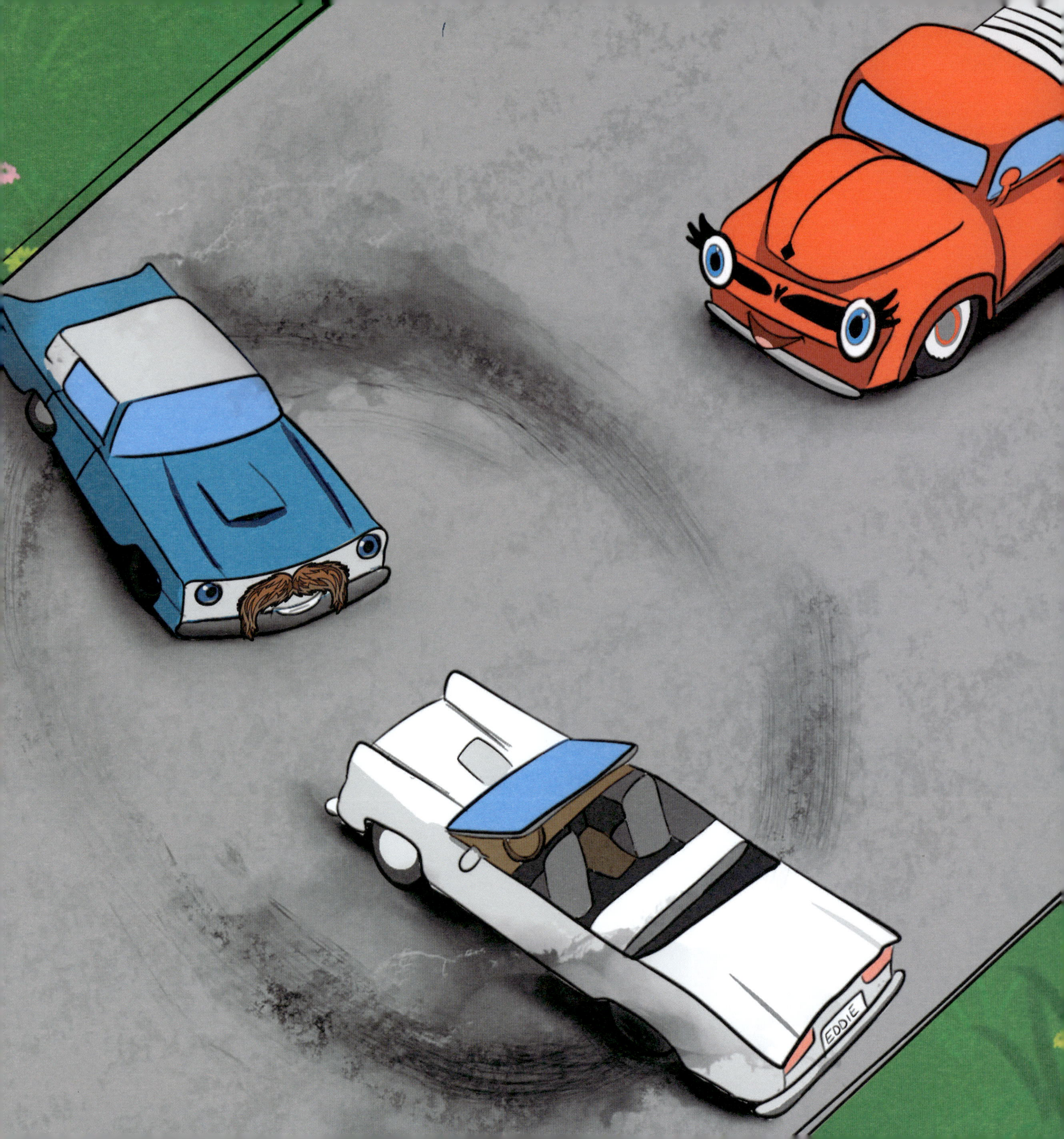
EDDIE

Rosie & Friends
Adventures of a FLOWER TRUCK

When she was done with her events Rosie would drive with the boys and watch while they did fun things like drive fast in circles in parking lots or try to race each other down long, empty country roads.

WHEEE! WHEEE!

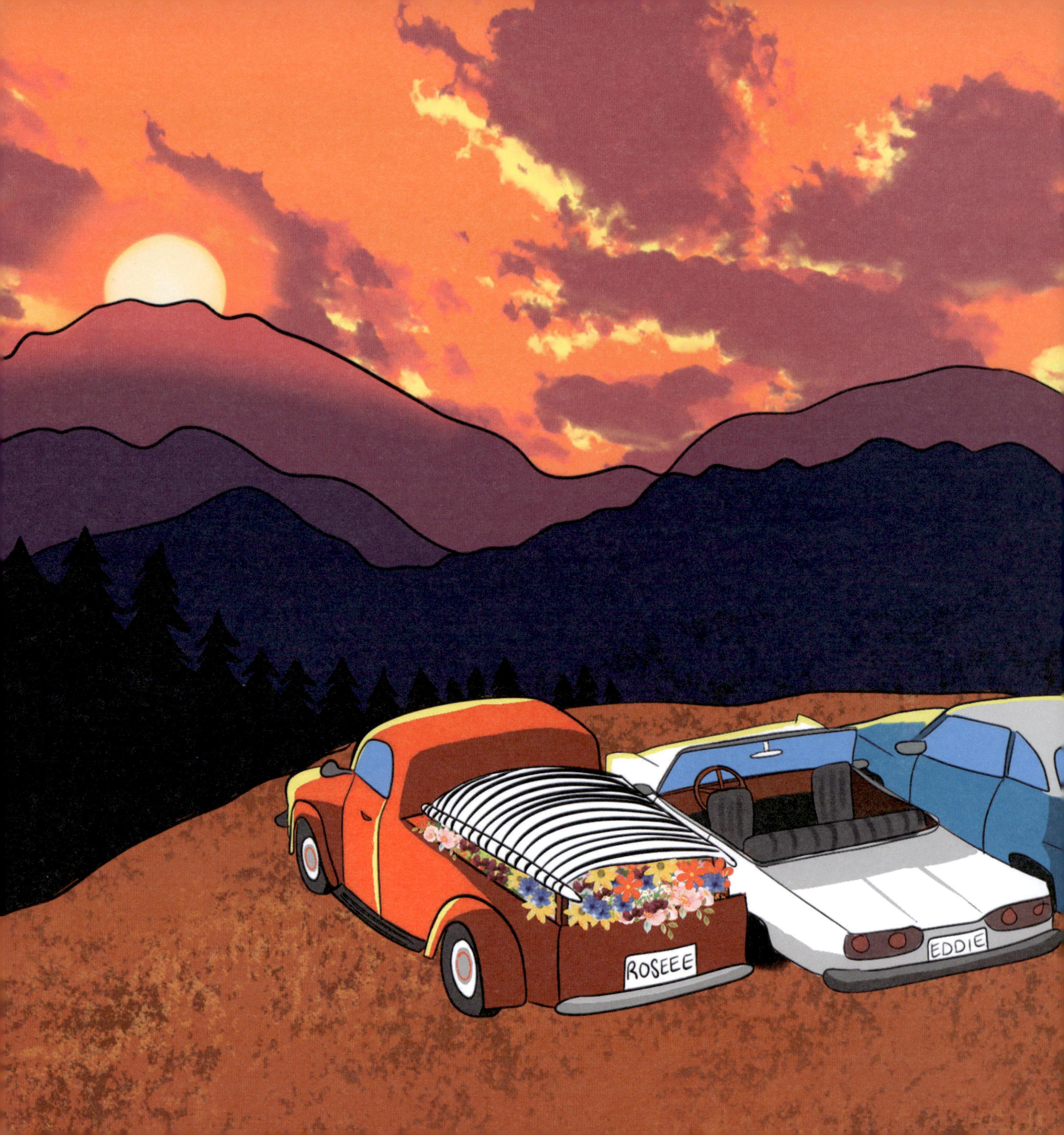
ROSEEE
EDDIE

Rosie & Friends
Adventures of a FLOWER TRUCK

They also liked to sit together at dusk and watch the sunset while sharing fun stories and laughing together. Then Dibo would head home and Rosie and Eddie would get tucked into their garage.

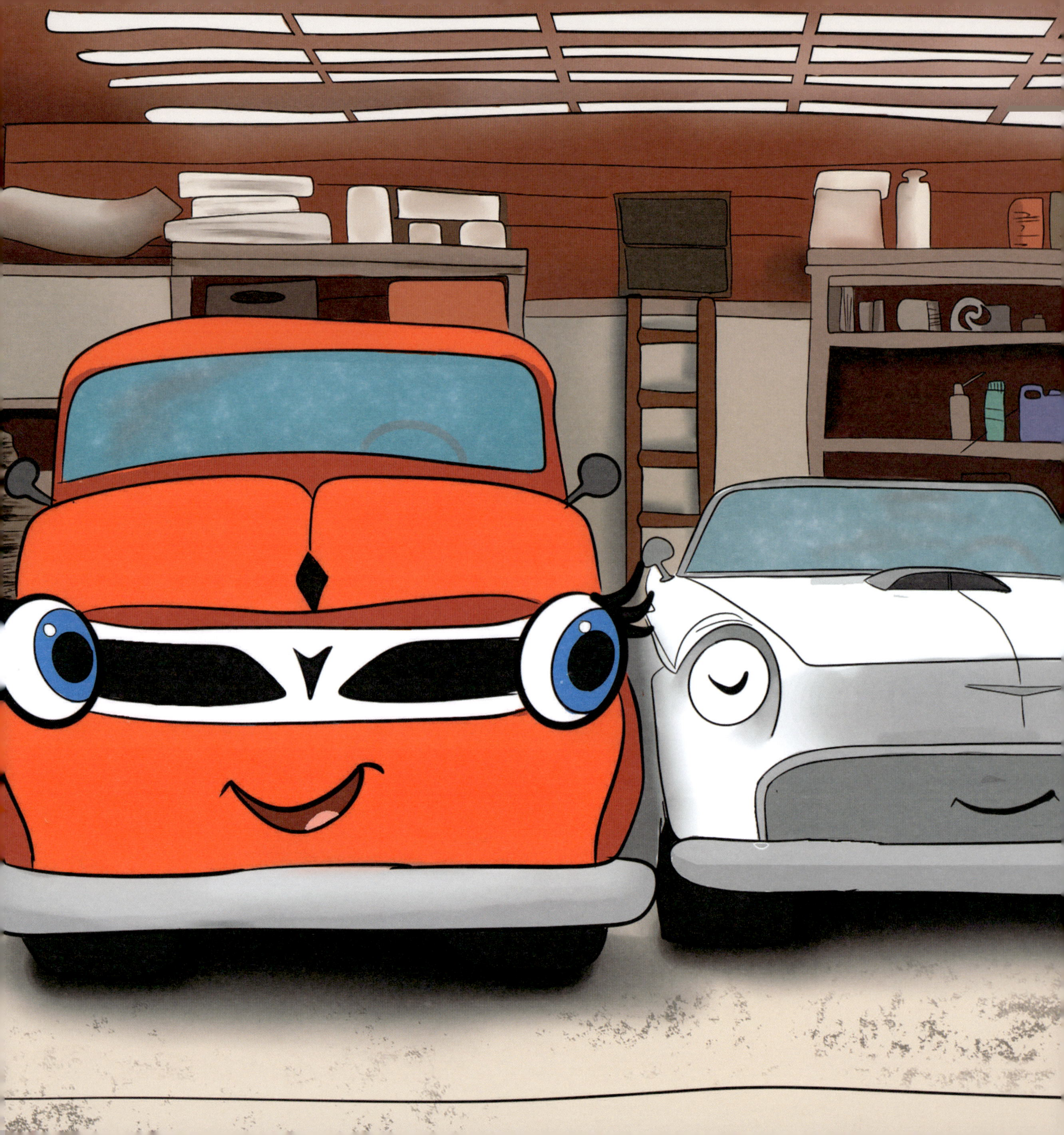

Rosie & Friends
Adventures of a FLOWER TRUCK

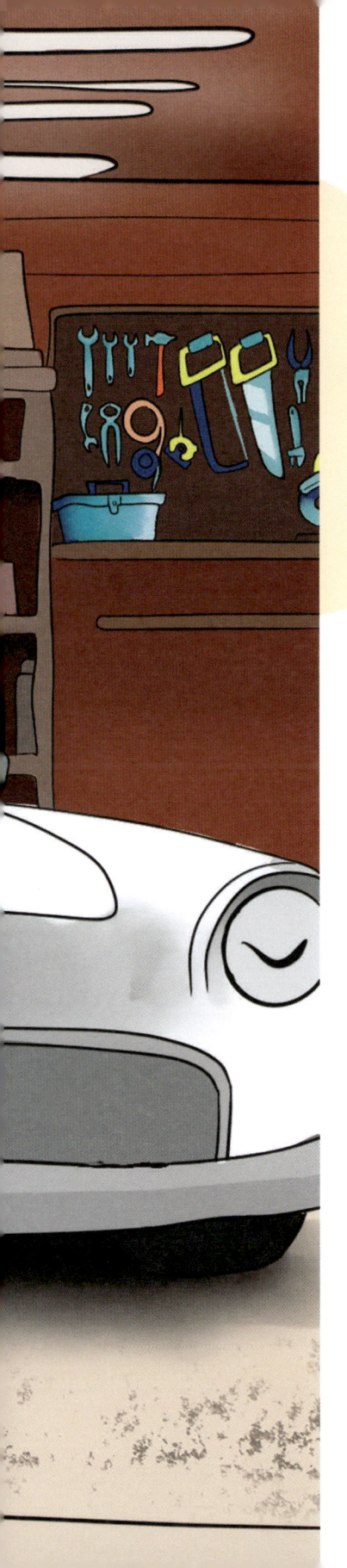

"Eddie, did you ever think we would have such a wonderful life with such good friends?" asked Rosie. "I'm so happy that you and Dibo and I are forever friends." But Eddie was already fast asleep, snoring away.

ZZZZZ!

That's okay, thought Rosie. *I know Eddie would agree!*

Every night, Rosie and Eddie were grateful for their fun-filled days and were ready to have new adventures in the morning.

Activity Pages

If you were a truck or a car, what kind would you be? What color would you be?

What adventures would you go on if you were a truck or car?

Rosie & Friends
Adventures of a FLOWER TRUCK

Would you like to be in a parade if you were a truck or car?

55

Activity Pages

In the illustration of Rosie in her first home, the old garage, there are many items on the floor and on the shelves. What items can you find?

Rosie & Friends
Adventures of a FLOWER TRUCK

Find the sounds in the story and say them out loud! The sounds are in capital letters.

Find Hank the fire engine. What kind of sound does his horn make? Hank would have a very deep voice.

Activity Pages

Rosie has friends Eddie and Dibo in this story. Who are your friends and what are their names? What do you like about your friends?

Rosie & Friends
Adventures of a FLOWER TRUCK

Can you find the Fu Manchu mustache on Dibo, the car? A Fu Manchu mustache on a person extends from under the nose past the corners of the mouth and grows downward past a clean shaven chin in two tapered lines of hair called tendrils. Sometimes it even extends past the jawline.

Meet the Author's Family

The author and members of the author's family are in the illustrations of this book. Can you find them?

Jessica, the author, and Patrick, her husband

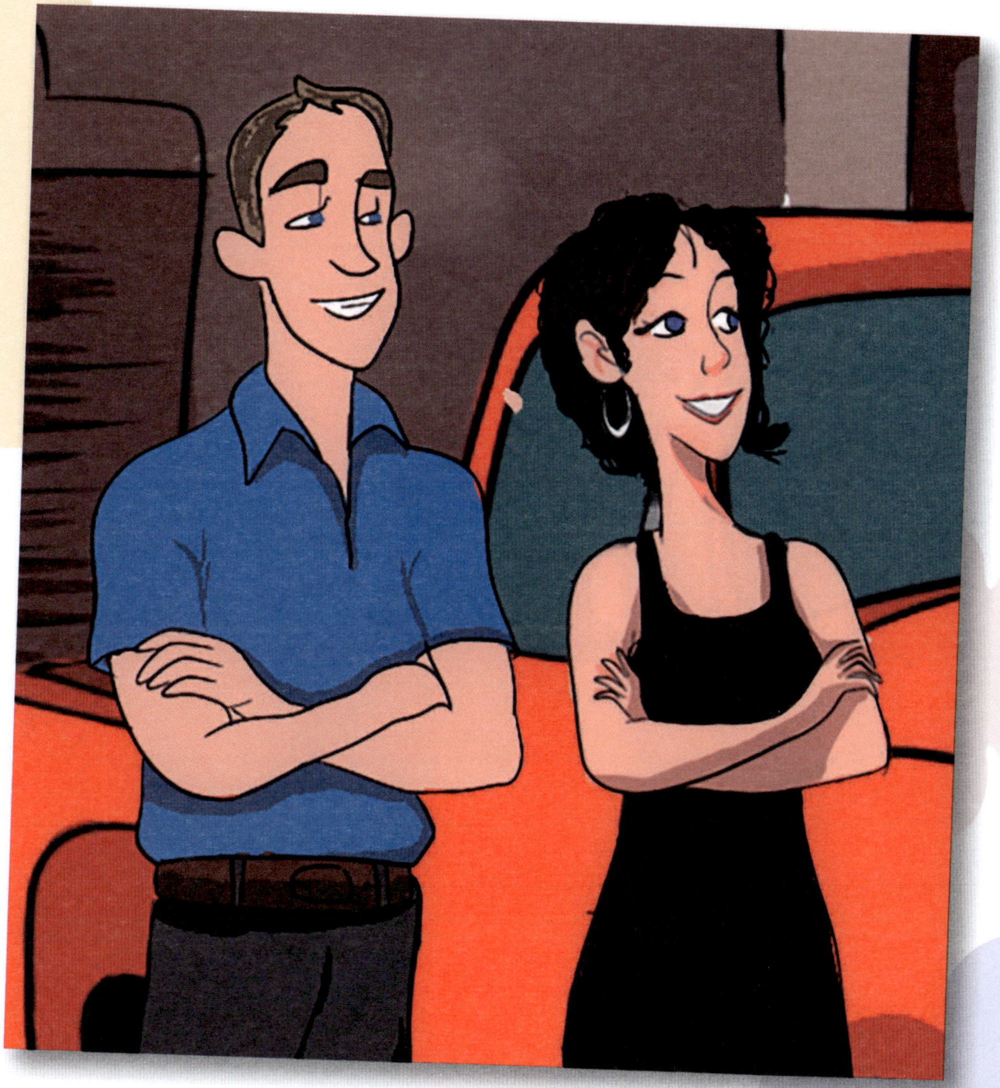

Ed and Rose,
Patrick's parents

Alex, Jessica and Patrick's son

Corine, Jessica's mother

Rose, Jessica's mother-in-law

Mazy, their black
Labrador Retriever dog

Winnie, their chocolate
Labrador Retriever dog

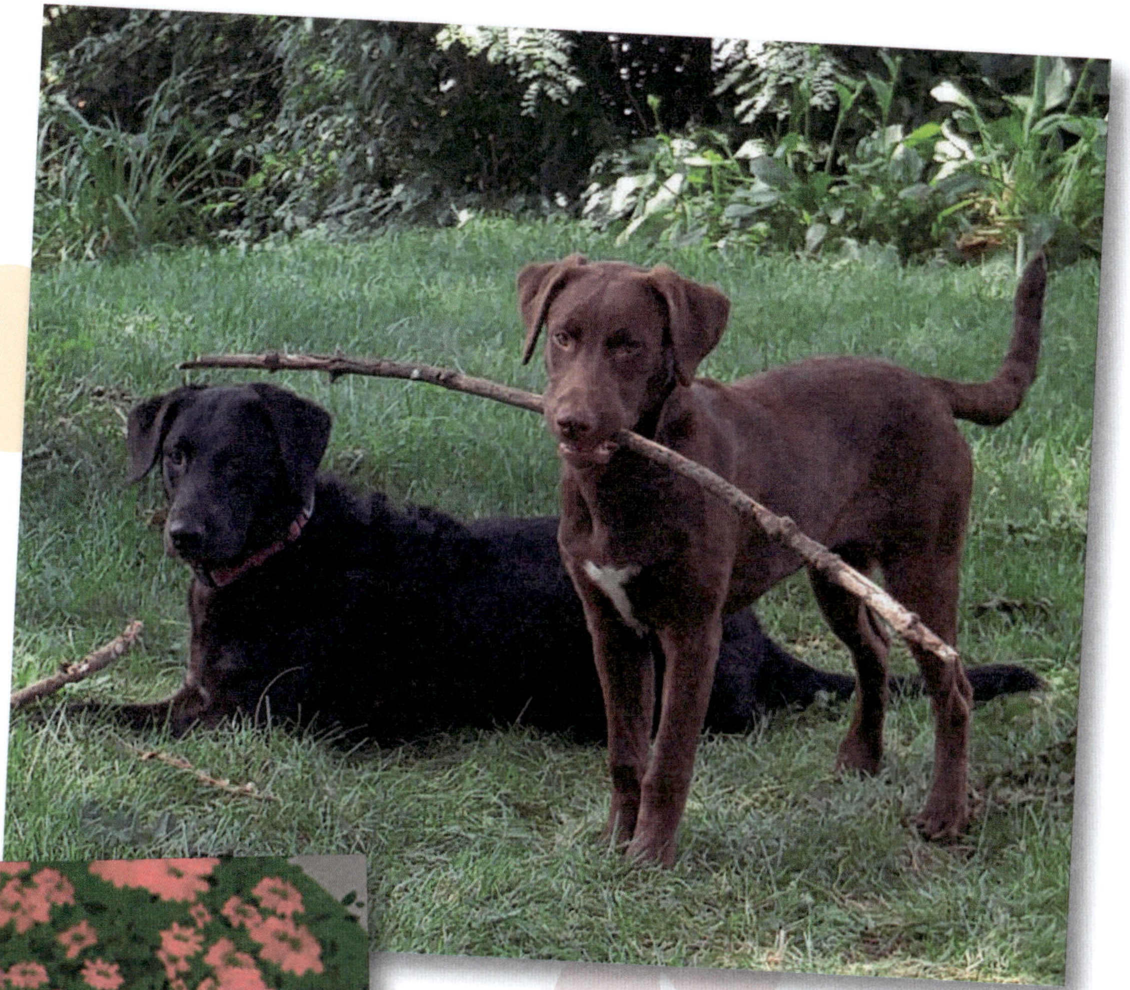

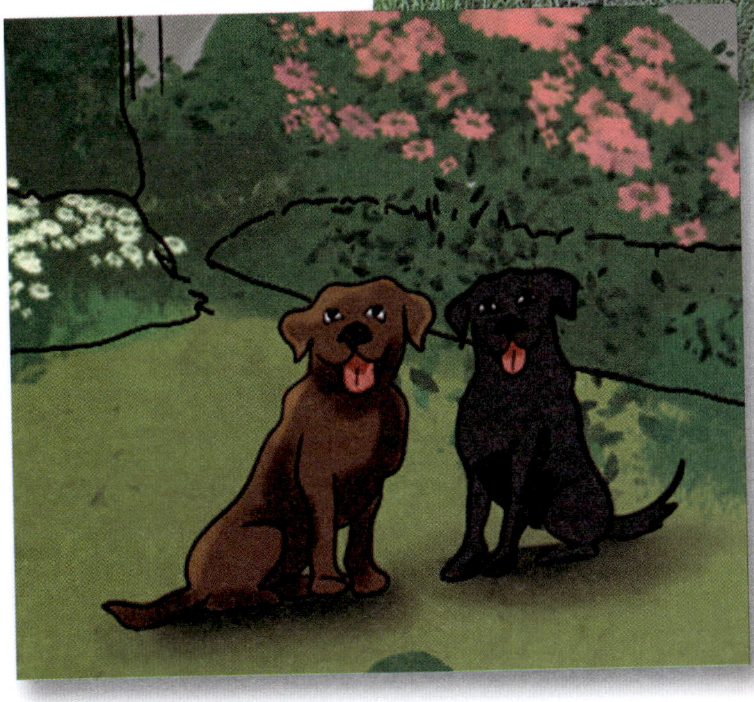

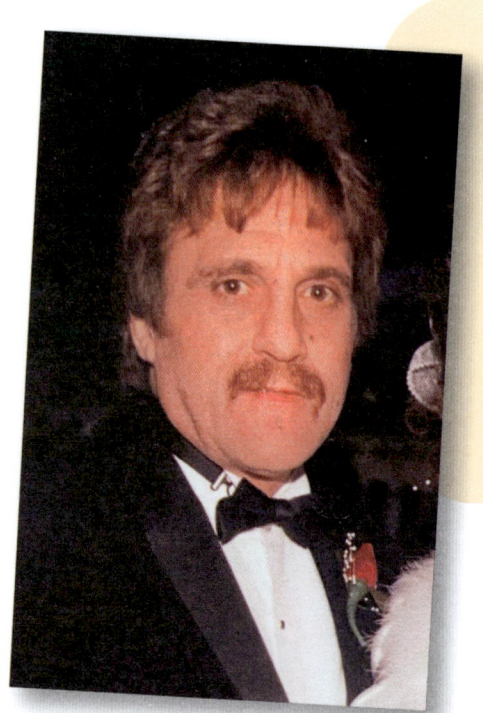

Eddie and Dibo are real people!

Rosie's Friends Eddie and Dibo

Eddie, the convertible, was created in memory of the author's father-in-law, Ed Maloy. Ed was a huge lover of antique cars. One antique car he owned was a 1956 white convertible Ford Thunderbird. Eddie in the story is white since Ed had white hair.

Dibo, the Chevy Impala, was created in memory of the author's father, Gary DiCarlo, who everyone knew as "Dibo". His favorite car was a 1963 Chevy Impala. Dibo always had a Fu Manchu mustache, so that was added to the Dibo car illustration.

Both men have passed away and the author knows they would love this story of Rosie and that they were included in it with the cars they loved so much named for them.

70

Meet a Flower Truck Named Rosie

This story about Rosie is sort of true. She is a 1953 Ford F100. She was in New York, alone in a garage and not driven. We found her for sale online and went up to New York to see her. We couldn't drive the truck yet so she had to be put on a trailer to get her to Pennsylvania. Patrick, my husband, did some work on her, including the tires and bumpers just like in the story. Patrick also built the flower bed part and my mom and I made the fabric cover. We named her Rosie because she's red (like a rose) and she sells flowers. Rosie is also Patrick's mom's name. Well, her name is Rose but his dad always called her Rosie so it's her nickname. We did ask her for permission before naming the truck. Rosie is very fun to

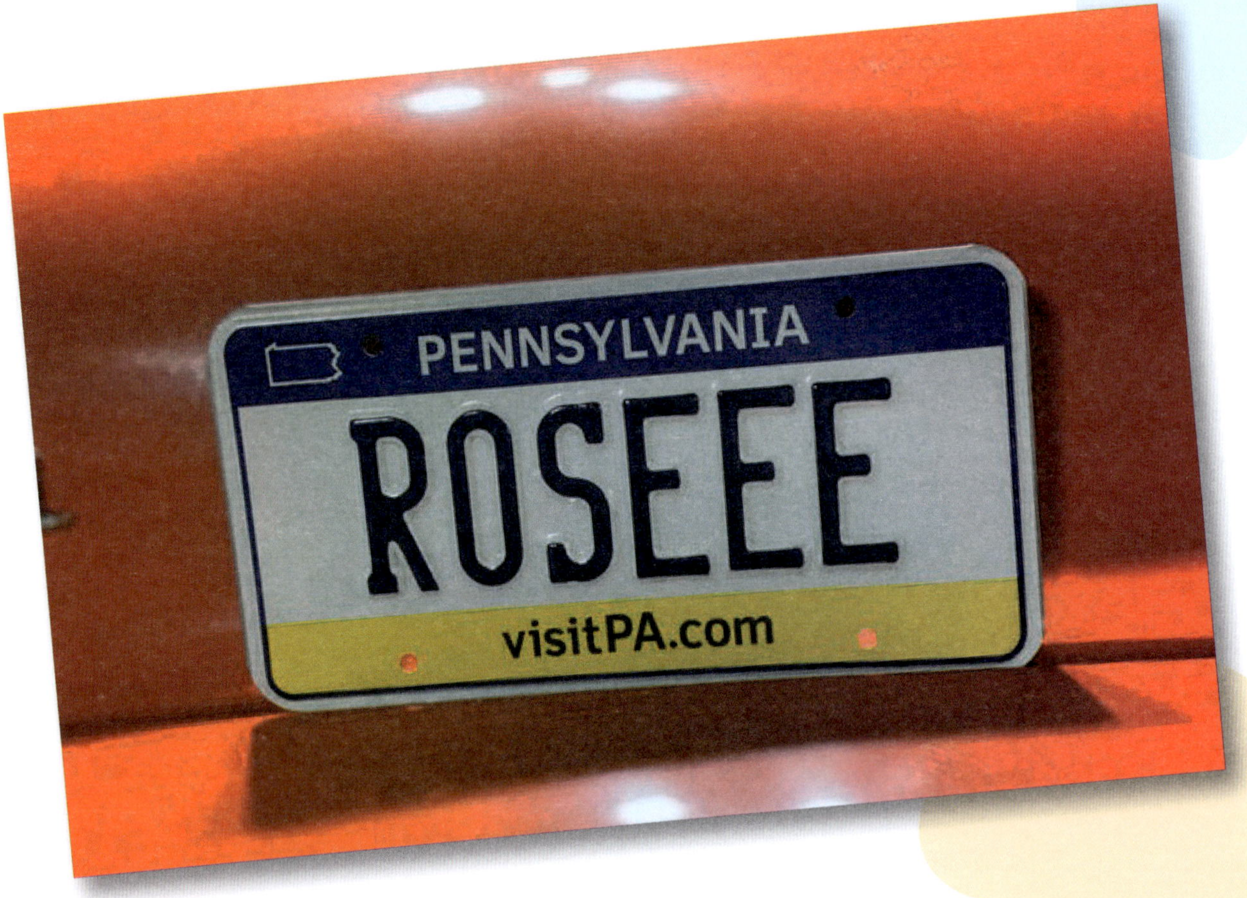
PENNSYLVANIA
ROSEEE
visitPA.com

drive, but can be tricky because she still has her original engine, which doesn't go very fast and is quite loud. She also has a funny sounding horn. I feel like Rosie really is magical, as she does bring joy to others, even just passing by people on the street. The flowers make it all extra special. I hope you enjoyed getting to know Rosie.

About the Author
Jessica Maloy

Jessica Maloy grew up in Mingo Junction, Ohio, moving to Pennsylvania, where she still lives, when she was 10 years old. As a child she enjoyed playing with dolls like Barbies. She loves flowers, animals and all things DIY (Do It Yourself).

When Jessica was in her 30s she came to the realization that she was physically strong. She was encouraged to compete in Powerlifting and with hard work she became very successful in her competitions. In her 4 years of competing she earned 12 World Records, 6 National Records and 24 Pennsylvania State Records. One of the benefits of these competitions was that she could show by example, and also spread the word, that girls can be strong. She often heard people comment that she was "strong for a girl", when "for a girl" was not necessary…both boys and girls can be strong. Jessica finds it very empowering to be a strong female. In her book she wanted Rosie to be strong and also feminine.

During the summer of 2020 with COVID and quarantine, Jessica was inspired by the idea of building "a cute little greenhouse" in her backyard. She loves designing and decorating and her husband, Patrick, is very handy and loves carpentry. They had a lot of fun putting the greenhouse together. That was the start of her business Palmyra Greenhouse. She knew it was meant to be! While she loves growing flowers and designing floral arrangements, her favorite part of the business is delivering flowers to people. Seeing the smiles on people's faces made her realize that she needed to get more flowers out to more people. A great way to get more flowers to more people was to create "Rosie". Patrick grew up in a family that loved antique cars and even helped his dad, Eddie, restore a 1964 ½ Ford Mustang when he was in middle school. So it wasn't difficult to talk him into the Flower Truck idea, especially using an old Ford truck. Eddie and Dibo, the cars in this story, are named after their fathers, both of whom have passed away. Both fathers are created into their favorite antique cars for the story. In this book, Eddie was Ed's nickname, Patrick's father, and Dibo is the nickname for Jessica's father, Gary. These special cars are friends of Rosie in this story.

    Jessica and her husband, Patrick, have one son, Alex. They live in Palmyra, Pennsylvania and share their home with 2 dogs and a cat.